TWELVE
LIES
Wives TELL
THEIR HUSBANDS

ALSO BY TIM & SHEILA RITER

Twelve Lies Husbands Tell Their Wives

BY TIM RITER

Twelve Lies You Hear in Church

Twelve Lies You Hear about the Holy Spirit

Just Leave God Out of It! (with David Timms)

TWELVE
LIES
Wives TELL
THEIR HUSBANDS

Tim & Sheila Riter

 LIFE JOURNEY®

Bringing Home the Message for Life

COOK COMMUNICATIONS MINISTRIES
Colorado Springs, Colorado • Paris, Ontario
KINGSWAY COMMUNICATIONS LTD
Eastbourne, England

Life Journey® is an imprint of
Cook Communications Ministries, Colorado Springs, CO 80918
Cook Communications, Paris, Ontario
Kingsway Communications, Eastbourne, England

TWELVE LIES WIVES TELL THEIR HUSBANDS
© 2005 by Tim and Sheila Riter

First Printing, 2005
Printed in United States of America
1 2 3 4 5 6 7 8 9 10 Printing/Year 09 08 07 06 05

Cover Design: BMB Design/Scott Johnson

Unless otherwise noted, Scripture quotations are taken from the HOLY BIBLE, NEW INTERNATIONAL VERSION®. Copyright © 1973, 1978, 1984 International Bible Society. Used by permission of Zondervan. Scripture quotations marked NLT are taken from the Holy Bible. New Living Translation copyright © 1996 by Tyndale Charitable Trust. Used by permission of Tyndale House Publishers. All rights reserved. Scripture quotations marked AB are taken from the *Amplified® Bible*, Copyright © 1954, 1958, 1962, 1964, 1965, 1987 by the Lockman Foundation. Used by permission. All rights reserved. Scripture quotations marked NKJV are taken from the New King James®. Copyright © 1882 by Thomas Nelson, Inc. Used by permission. All rights reserved. Scripture quotations marked NRSV are taken from the *New Revised Standard Version of the Bible*, copyrighted by the Division of Christian Education of the National Council of the Churches of Christ in the United States of America, and are used by permission.
Italics in Scripture references are placed by the authors for emphasis.

Library of Congress Cataloging-in-Publication Data

Riter, Tim, 1948-
    Twelve lies wives tell their husbands / By Tim and Sheila Riter.
        p. cm.
    Includes bibliographical references.
    ISBN 0-7814-4135-8 (pbk.)
    1. Wives–Religious life. 2. Interpersonal communication–Religious aspects–Christianity. 3. Marriage–Religious aspects–Christianity. 4. Women–Psychology. I. Riter, Sheila. II. Title.
BV4528.15.R57 2005
248.8'431–dc22
                            2004029292

With great appreciation to all those who have spoken truth into our lives, who have demonstrated integrity in their lives, and who have shared their stories with us. The line may not be fresh, but it's true: this book would have been impossible without you.

Our gratitude, respect, and thanks to Vickie Barton, Dwayne Benson, Rosalie and Stan Campbell, Jerry Christensen, Susy Flory, Teri Garcia, Guy Glimpse, Jeannie Harmon, Fritz Moga, Curt Peterson, Jim Price, Thelma and Herb Read, Chris Schaal, John Southwood, Chris Houghton (counselor), Carl Mascarella (counselor), Celebrate Recovery at Cornerstone Community Church in Wildomar, California, the boys at New Life, New Hope Recovery at Canyon Lake Community Church in Canyon Lake, California, and to many others who wish to remain anonymous.

Contents

Introduction: The Truth, the Whole Truth, and Nothing
but the Truth *9*

Lie 1: I Love You Just the Way You Are
The Truth about Acceptance *21*

Lie 2: I'll Always Respect You—as Long as You Deserve It
The Truth about Respect and Appreciation *33*

Lie 3: I'll Love You for Richer or for Poorer
The Truth about Financial Partnership *47*

Lie 4: You Aren't My Boss
The Truth about Submission *61*

Lie 5: I'll Never Be Unfaithful to You
The Truth about Faithfulness *79*

Lie 6: Nothing's Wrong; I'm Just Fine
The Truth about Direct Communication *93*

Lie 7: I Don't Need Your Help; I Can Take Care of It
The Truth about Communicating Needs *105*

Lie 8: We Just Don't Have Anything in Common Anymore
The Truth about Personal Intimacy *113*

Lie 9: Do I Look Good in This Dress? I Really Want to Know
The Truth about Honesty, Criticism, and Affirmation 125

Lie 10: You Never Talk to Me
The Truth about Conversation *135*

Lie 11: Not Tonight, Dear; I Have a Headache
The Truth about Sexual Intimacy *147*

Lie 12: You Need to Grow Up and Face Responsibility
The Truth about Adventure *163*

Notes *177*

Readers' Guide *181*

Introduction

The Truth, the Whole Truth, and Nothing but the Truth

*Instead, speaking the truth in love, we will in
all things grow up into ... Christ.*
—Ephesians 4:15

The wife says, "I love you just the way you are," but after the wedding ceremony she embarks on a domestic reclamation project to transform her husband into the person she really desires. Her acts of appreciation to win his heart just disappear.

The wife tells her husband, "I'll always respect you," but then adds, "as long as you deserve it," thus excusing herself from keeping her promise.

The wife vows, "I'll love you for richer or for poorer," but then hides expenditures and feels insecure when financial difficulties arise.

The wife says, "I'll never be unfaithful to you," but then carries on an affair of the imagination with a coworker for several years.

The wife says, "Not tonight, dear; I have a headache," but the reason she doesn't want her husband to touch her is because of an insensitive comment he made several days earlier.

The wife says, "Honey, I don't need your help; I'll take care of it," when she really wants her husband to jump in and work alongside her.

The wife says, "Do I look good in this dress? I really want

to know," when what she wants is a compliment instead of a fashion critique.

The wife says, "Nothing's wrong; I'm just fine," when in truth she feels ready to leave the marriage.

Wives and husbands, have you ever experienced some form of lying? Some form of telling less than the full truth? Perhaps it took the form of misdirection—she shaded the truth just enough to point away from reality. Perhaps she told just part of the truth; enough to sound good, but mixed with enough untruth to protect her.

Husbands, have you become frustrated with some of the lies your wife tells you? Do you wonder why she doesn't just "tell it like it is"? Have you seen the companionship you yearn for damaged by dishonesty and deception?

Wives, do you wonder why you mislead your husband? Do you find it difficult to tell "the truth, the whole truth, and nothing but the truth"? Do you long for a safe environment that makes it easier to be honest? And, have you become frustrated at your seeming inability to tell the full truth to your husband?

This book and its companion, *Twelve Lies Husbands Tell Their Wives*, may provide a solution.

Husbands, we'll help you learn what she really means and how to make it easier for her to be fully truthful. Wives, we'll help you understand the impact your lack of candor can have on your husband. Then, we'll help you build an environment of safe transparency, one that gives us all the opportunity to make the most of the marriage God has placed us in.

These two books operate on the thesis that moving beyond the untruths we tell will enhance our marriages. Some untruths are humorous; some are serious. Some are direct lies; others never say anything directly untrue, but they intentionally mislead. The more truth we tell, the closer we can get to one another. The less truth we tell, the further apart we move. Our desire for closeness determines how honest we will be.

We realize that many husbands will want to get right to the lies that their wives tell, read them, and say, "See, I told you so! You've got to change!"

Please resist that temptation! We encourage every reader to begin by looking within and asking, "What do I do to contribute to the problem? What can I do to increase truth in our marriage?" Let's make this a time of personal change.

But who are we? Why should you listen to anything we say? Mostly, because we've been there. We've gone through a number of struggles, most of them coming from telling partial truths or hiding things. We've both been in recovery groups. Through painful discovery, we've learned that truth sets us free (see John 8:32), and that any form of dishonesty enslaves us. We're willing to share our journey with you, some of the mistakes we've made, and what God has done in our lives. Our experiences include more than twenty years in local church ministry, so we've seen the effects of untruths in the lives of others. We've had to pick up the pieces of a broken relationship that results from a lack of full honesty. Tim also teaches communications at a Christian university in our area and does some speaking along with writing books.

In addition, a number of friends and associates have shared their stories with us and allowed us to use them in these books. Generally, using a last name represents a true identity. When a first name only is used, then the identity is disguised in several significant details. Now, before we get into the lies, we need to have a clear understanding of the importance of truth.

Cherish Truth

Few would dispute the concept that behavior follows values. Or to say it another way, we only act upon that which we truly believe. We examine the options, determine which ones best express what we view as most important, and then take action based on our evaluation.

That means if we want to live in truth, we must value it and the benefits it brings more than we value what untruth brings. We therefore can increase our TQ—or "truth quotient"—by increasing how much we value truth. We decide that the benefits of telling the truth outweigh the benefits of misleading people.

God will work in the truth (see John 8:32), but we can tie his hands in a lie. That can be a tough process for many of us! We've lived in various forms of lies for so long that we've become accustomed to them. Often, we don't even realize we're saying them. That's why we've been specific with the lies, to give an "Aha!" moment. "Yeah, I've said that before. And now that I think about it, I really wasn't being honest." Or, "*They* weren't being honest." Truth cuts in both directions. And although we encourage you, the reader, to look at yourself rather than at others, we can all benefit from recognizing the untruths we hear and speak.

So, let's see why we should cherish truth and move away from untruth.

TRUTH REFLECTS THE FATHER

First, truth inseparably flows from the nature of all three Persons of the Godhead. In times of difficulty, David called on God for help and referred to him as a sheltering rock and a protective fortress. Verse 5 of Psalm 31 reveals why David felt he could trust God for help: "Into your hands I commit my spirit; redeem me, O LORD, *the God of truth*."

God the Father has truth inextricably wound up in who he is. He can no more tell an untruth than we can live on this earth without sin.

TRUTH REFLECTS THE SON

We find the same connection between truth and the Son. On the evening before his arrest, Jesus told his disciples that he would soon be leaving. They wanted to go with him, but he had spoken of his death. They then talked about going to the Father, and Jesus described both himself and his mission in a familiar statement: "I *am* the way and *the truth* and the life. No one comes to the Father except through me" (John 14:6).

Rather than just *telling* the truth, as we may do, Jesus *is* truth. Truth is a part of his identity.

Truth played an equally central role in his ministry. In Matthew alone, Jesus began teaching with the phrase "I tell you the truth" a total of thirty times. With some repetitions, in all the gospel accounts, he used that phrase seventy-nine times. Why? He valued truth and wanted his hearers to be able to trust him to deliver it.

TRUTH REFLECTS THE SPIRIT

The third Person of the Godhead also has truth in his character. While continuing on the subject of his imminent departure, Jesus told his followers they would benefit from it, since his leaving would allow the Spirit to come. Who was this Spirit, and what would he do? "But when he, *the Spirit of truth*, comes, he will *guide you into all truth*. He will not speak on his own; he will speak only what he hears, and he will tell you what is yet to come" (John 16:13). Just like the Father and the Son, the Spirit's identity connects with truth. John defines the Spirit as the "Spirit of truth" three times from 14:17 to 16:13.

One of the Spirit's functions is to lead us into the truth. He wants us all to have more truth in our lives, and he works with us to achieve that goal.

So when we move into truth, we move closer to God because God is truth. When we move away from truth, however, we move closer to the realm of Satan.

UNTRUTH REFLECTS SATAN

In a raucous encounter in John 8, Jesus made a very clear contrast in the sources of truth and untruth.

> "You belong to your father, the *devil*, and you want to carry out your father's desire. He was a murderer from the beginning, not holding to the truth, for *there is no truth in him*. When he lies, he speaks his native language, for *he is a liar and the father of lies*. Yet because I tell the truth, you do not believe me! Can any of you

prove me guilty of sin? If I am telling the truth,
why don't you believe me?" (John 8:44-46)

Just as truth reflects the character and identity of God, so
untruth reflects the character and identity of the Devil. Think
about the implications. Not only do untruths damage our relationships, they also move us closer to their source. Each time
we allow a misperception, we make a spiritual decision. Do we
wish to live in the realm of God, or of Satan? Granted, we don't
typically think of it in those terms, but we can't separate the
behavior from its source.

Understand the Benefits of Truth

Everything God tells us to do will bring benefits to us, if
we are obedient enough to do it. His commands make for a
better life for us. But often we lie because we think it will
benefit us more than God's truth. We need to deeply believe
that truth holds more benefits than untruth. Let's survey some
of those benefits.

INTIMACY WITH GOD

Leading the list of benefits is intimacy with God, and it
flows directly from what we just explored. In 2 John 1:1-7, the
apostle John returned to the subject of truth. To John, truth
went beyond accurate statements—it encapsulated the Person
of God.

> The elder, to the chosen lady and her children,
> whom I love in the *truth*—and not I only, but
> also all who know the *truth*—because of the
> *truth*, which lives in us and will be with us
> forever: Grace, mercy and peace from God the
> Father and from Jesus Christ, the Father's Son,
> will be with us in *truth* and love. It has given
> me great joy to find some of your children
> walking in the *truth*, just as the Father
> commanded us. And now, dear lady, I am not
> writing you a new command but one we have
> had from the beginning. I ask that we love one

another. And this is love: that we walk in obedience to his commands. As you have heard from the beginning, his command is that you walk in love. Many *deceivers*, who do not acknowledge Jesus Christ as coming in the flesh, have gone out into the world. Any such person is *the deceiver and the antichrist*.

Like his quotes of Jesus in his gospel account, John also contrasted walking in truth with deceit. And he hammered his readers on the point that truth and God go hand in glove. When we walk in truth (accuracy), we walk with *the* truth (the Father and the Son).

So, as we live in the fullness of truth, we increase our intimacy with God. Not a bad way to begin our pursuit of truth!

SPIRITUAL GROWTH

A commitment to truth also opens the doors to growth in spiritual maturity. In Ephesians 4:11–16, Paul explored how our connection to others in the church allows us to grow in Christ. Verse 15 provides a vital part of that growth: "Instead, *speaking the truth* in love, *we will in all things grow up* into him who is the Head, that is, Christ."

Lovingly telling the truth allows us to grow. The converse: when we don't speak the truth in love, we retard our spiritual growth.

SPIRITUAL PROTECTION

We all face multitudes of temptations every day of our lives. In Ephesians 6:10–18, Paul explored the reality of the spiritual battle. He encouraged us to be strong in the Lord by using the spiritual armor that God provides. At the center of the armor lies truth: "Stand firm then, with *the belt of truth buckled around your waist*, with the breastplate of righteousness in place" (v. 14).

The belt holds the armor together. Take away truth, and we lose the armor. Buckle on truth, and we take a major step in dealing with the spiritual battles we encounter.

I (Tim) allowed myself to get caught up in looking at some sexually inappropriate Internet sites for about a year. And although I always knew it was wrong, in my mind I minimized the damage. Only when I accepted the truth of the damage it brought to my walk with God, my character, and my marriage could I begin to experience victory.

Truth brings spiritual protection to us by reminding us of reality.

FREEDOM

Jesus gave the classic statement on truth, again in the gospel of John: "To the Jews who had believed him, Jesus said, 'If you hold to my teaching, you are really my disciples. Then you will *know the truth, and the truth will set you free*'" (John 8:31–32).

In the context, Jesus was talking about being free from slavery to sin. What truth would free us? That answer has several layers. Obviously, we need to know Jesus, the truth. But we also need to know the truth that Jesus died to pay the penalty for our sins. We can be forgiven, but only through Jesus' death for us. And we need to know the truth that we can access the Father only through the Son. (See John 14:6.)

But we can't separate the truth about Jesus from our valuing truth in our daily lives. Putting the truth of God's Word in one compartment of our lives and living each day as though that truth doesn't exist won't do us any good. The more we live in truth, the closer we get to God. So, truth allows us freedom to build more intimacy with him. It seems as if that theme keeps coming back, doesn't it? Truth and closeness with God go together.

We hope this section has given you a glimpse of how truth benefits our lives. Once we grasp the benefits, we will value truth more and more.

Aim for Transparency

If living in the truth benefits us, and if living in untruth damages us, then any wise person would commit to living in full truth, right? Well, we like the idea, but living it out is pretty tough. Besides, living in truth sounds a bit lofty, not very practical. To give us a way to define what it means to live in "full truth," we describe it as *appropriate transparency.* Being transparent means we're an open book; we don't speak direct lies; we don't mislead even with truthful statements; we don't hide things that we should disclose.

But transparency needs to be appropriate, and we need to establish two major limits.

First we need to ask, does the person have a right to know this? Some information is validly private. In our marriages, we don't particularly need to tell our spouses every detail of our lives before we met. I (Tim) found that mentioning I had dated a particular individual before Sheila's and my marriage didn't necessarily improve our relationship! Also, information we have about other people often shouldn't be disclosed without their permission.

Second, do we speak in love? Paul gave that injunction in Ephesians 4:15. It's possible to speak the truth but damage others with what we share, to speak the truth but serve our interests instead of those of our spouse.

We realize these two limits are loose and that exactly how we express them will vary. But we do need to ask the questions before we choose to reveal truth and then genuinely grapple with what God would have us do in a given situation. Why? Transparency forms the basis of intimacy.

TRANSPARENCY: ALREADY A REALITY WITH GOD

Isn't it amazing how we sometimes think we can fool others! Even more, how we think we can fool God. Hebrews 4:12-13 lets us know that to God, we are already fully transparent.

> For the word of God is living and active. Sharper than any double-edged sword, it penetrates even to dividing soul and spirit, joints and marrow; it judges the thoughts and attitudes of the heart. Nothing in all creation is

hidden from God's sight. Everything is uncov-
ered and laid bare before the eyes of him to
whom we must give account.

God knows our every thought, attitude, and act. Yet he
still loves and accepts us. He may not always like what we do,
but he does love us! We can be fully honest with God; we don't
have to hide anything since he already knows it. And, knowing
that he'll continue to love and accept us makes it easier to fully
tell the truth to him. Being honest with him won't ever hurt us.

TRANSPARENCY: A GOAL FOR MARRIAGES

In the old *Lone Ranger* TV series, each episode began
with the statement, "Return with us now to those thrilling days
of yesteryear." For this section, let's return to the very beginning of marriage to discover God's heart for us. In Genesis 2,
God decreed that it wasn't good for his newly created man to
be alone, and that none of the animals he'd created could fill
that void in Adam's life. (See vv. 18–21.) So God took a rib from
the man and created a woman.

Now, notice the blueprint for marriage set forth in
verses 23–25:

> The man said, "This is now bone of my bones
> and flesh of my flesh; she shall be called
> 'woman,' for she was taken out of man." For this
> reason a man will leave his father and mother
> and be united to his wife, and they will become
> one flesh. The man and his wife were both
> naked, and they felt no shame.

Three principles stand out from this passage. First, the
intimacy that both husbands and wives long for flows from
Creation. We have a God-given desire to be reunited since we
came from the same flesh.

Second, that longing begins to find its fulfillment in
marriage as the two individuals become one.

Third, marriage involves nakedness—literal as well as
figurative. Clothing keeps others from seeing the parts of us we

want to keep hidden. (There comes a point in our lives when we wear clothing to do others a favor!) But if marriage reunites us as one body, then should we hide things from our own body?

We believe our marriages should move in the direction of spiritual and emotional transparency, because that best expresses God's blueprint. Will we be perfectly transparent? No. Does our inability to be fully transparent excuse us from making it a goal? Again, no.

In our marriages, are we "naked and without shame"? We'd like to suggest that we can't easily do the first without the second and that the ability to do both comes from God himself. Marriage was designed to be a safe place where we can grow into transparency without guilt and insecurity. How do we combine these two?

That's important, because often when we express a failing, we expect to face hostility and judgment. Since few of us like pain, we avoid sharing. We shade the truth, tell only part of the truth, tell outright lies. Now, the plea of self-defense doesn't justify what we do, and it damages our character, our intimacy with God, and our marriage.

God demonstrates a response to truth telling that eliminates the need for deception: grace. He confronts the untruth and loves the sinner even as he hates the sin. Let's go back to the Hebrews passage that revealed that God knows everything about us, yet still loves and accepts us. We can be fully honest with God, knowing he won't ever stop loving and accepting us.

The combination of God seeing us fully and still loving us provides a pattern for how we can increase transparency in our marriages. When we know that our honesty won't unduly hurt us, we can move closer to it. We begin to realize that our honesty will often bring pain, but not as much as untruth.

That means we can help our mates to be transparent. As we provide a safe harbor, we make it easier for them not to have to mislead us.

That doesn't mean we ignore sin and pretend we're not hurt by it. But we continue to love our spouses as God loves us. We continue to accept our mates as God accepts us. Rather than allowing the truth to become a dividing wall, we choose to work together as a team. We realize that truth sets us free, and when we are free, we can then work on issues that need attention.

We realize that speaking the full truth doesn't eliminate consequences. If a husband confesses to multiple adulterous affairs, his confession doesn't clear the slate. Damage has been done, and it must be addressed before restoration can be attempted. Even then, the wound may be too deep for reconciliation.

But as we love and accept one another, we build an environment that encourages full honesty. That full honesty will benefit our marriages in multiple ways.

Realize also that for those of us who have allowed untruth to slip into our lives, who have kept things from our spouses to protect them or us, this journey to full truth is a process. We don't become instantly and totally transparent. We'll knowingly not tell the full truth at times. We'll discover areas that we may not have really understood as an issue of truth. Despite these setbacks, we can focus on the direction of the journey toward truth, toward God. We won't let the failings derail us, but we'll make them less frequent!

As we continue to walk with truth, we'll become intoxicated with the freedom that truth brings. We'll soar in joy as we experience new intimacy with our spouses. We'll stand in awe of the closeness we develop with God. And we'll wonder why we waited so long to pursue transparency.

Now, let's begin the journey into truth by exploring *Twelve Lies Wives Tell Their Husbands.*

Lie 1

I Love You Just the Way You Are

The Truth about Acceptance

Krista couldn't wait to tell Meggie the news about the guy she'd met at church, and she gushed as they sat down with their double lattes. "Joel is *so* cool. He just moved into town with that big tech company. He's in some kind of management; I didn't want to push too much!

"But he's tall, kinda good looking, he loves the Lord and is real athletic. You know that big cliff over by the river? He's already climbed it—all by himself. I get scared just looking at it!"

"Gosh, he sounds like Mr. Perfect! The guy has to have some flaws, doesn't he?"

"Just little ones. He's a little quiet, but I can draw him out. And, he spends a lot of time with some new friends from work; I think they play sports a lot. And, this is gonna sound picky, but his car really needs a washing. But, he's a bachelor, and you know guys: the original slobs.

"But he doesn't have any problems that I can't fix. I just have to work on him a little, and he'll become a real Stepford husband."

The relationship did continue, and over the next several months it deepened as well. Then, while on a picnic at the river, Joel asked Krista to marry him. She paused for a moment and said, "Joel, I am so glad God brought you into my life. You're just the man I've always wanted, and just the man I thought I'd never find. I love you so much, just the way you are. I would be honored to become your wife."

And with the exchange of the rings, she began the changing process. Joel's quiet demeanor led Krista to work harder at getting him to talk more. She encouraged him to share his feelings and thoughts, and grew frustrated when he had nothing to say. She tried to get him to spend less time with his friends so the two of them could be alone. She kept her "gal pals" but felt threatened when he went out with his "buds." She nagged him to keep their belongings in better repair. That dirty car went along with a weed-filled lawn and rusted-out tools, things that bothered Krista and that she was determined to get Joel to change.

Joel made sure they went to their church each week, but Krista wanted him to read the same devotional book that she read every day. He would—sometimes—but they got out of sync and couldn't stay together. She began to wonder about his commitment to Christ.

But most of all, she pressured him to give up sports, especially the rock climbing. "Joel, you're a married man now. It's time to settle down and act like one. You have responsibilities here, and if you get hurt I can't do everything."

The Lie

Krista truly viewed Joel as a catch. His admirable qualities greatly overshadowed his flaws. And when she responded to his proposal by saying he was just the man she'd always dreamed of, she thought she spoke the truth. What she meant was that he had all the raw material she needed to craft him into the husband she yearned for.

Unfortunately, Joel took her words at face value; he believed that she loved him just as he was. Right then. Kind of like God loves his children—unconditionally. That's the marriage he yearned for. Krista didn't really understand why he thought she had lied when she said, "I love you just the way you are."

On the Receiving End

Joel had never been troubled by a huge ego, but he did think of himself as a pretty decent guy, and he thought Krista shared his view. He knew he wasn't as good as some, but like most, he thought he was a little above average. He listened to Krista, worked hard, and tried to please her. And since he truly accepted Krista as she was, he hoped she would accept him just the way he was. All in all, he expected a fairly smooth life with his new wife.

Krista's dissatisfaction took him completely by surprise. Her subtle suggestions grew into sporadic digs and then almost constant nagging. Like many men, he couldn't express his feelings to Krista very well, but he began to feel unappreciated. She seemed to ignore the good things he did and talked only about his failings. He began to feel that he couldn't do anything to please her.

His feelings of being unappreciated and his frustration at not being able to please her caused him to wonder if she truly loved him: *Does she feel attracted to me, or to the person she wants me to be? I just don't get it. I've got an MBA, I get great reviews at work, but at home she's never satisfied with what I do.*

As a result of Krista's complaining and his inability to articulate his feelings, Joel began to withdraw conversationally. When he did share something, Krista tended to get critical about it, so he just quit giving her that chance. "Burn me once, shame on you; burn me twice, shame on me" became his philosophy.

More significantly, he backed off on the relationship altogether. He explained it to his work buddy Tom. "I love Krista, and I'm committed to our marriage. I'll never leave her; I'll never be unfaithful in any way. But I want someone, no, I need someone, who accepts me as I am, who doesn't want to change everything about me, who doesn't focus on what I do wrong. I just can't take the rejection I get from her. If I wrap my life around her, and all I get is criticism, her constant pushing me to change, it hurts too much. I need to protect myself; I can't be so vulnerable anymore. Besides, we're not talking about sin areas. She wants to change who I am."

Behind the Lie

One counselor suggested that Krista wanted to control Joel, to shape him into her ideal. That certainly seemed to describe their relationship. But there was a deeper issue involved: her strong need for security. The more she was able to control Joel, the more secure she felt in the relationship. If she could predict his behavior, she could feel more confident and relaxed.

Krista did love Joel deeply and truly wanted him to become his very best. The problem came from whose definition of "best" was being used. Joel felt fairly satisfied with himself. Sure, he could always grow, and he wanted to. But he longed for Krista to accept him as the unique person he was. After all, his quirks helped shape his identity.

But Krista thought she knew better how Joel could become better, and her plan for him included a long list of change points. She wanted him to improve his clothes selection. He liked to dress casually; shorts and T-shirts made up most of his wardrobe away from work. But she liked him in Dockers more than jeans and would only buy those for him.

She cherished her female friends and got together regularly with them for Bunco and Starbucks. But she resented the time he spent playing sports with his guy friends. Joel thought she scheduled "family" activities whenever he tried to get with his "buds." She wanted him to go to "chick flicks" with her, but complained when he wanted her to watch sports with him.

When she first met Joel, Krista loved his adventurous spirit. He'd done some traveling, wilderness hiking, and rock climbing. His slightly dangerous edge increased his appeal to her. But now she wanted safe weekend activities, like going on picnics and visiting the zoo. Camping in private campgrounds with pools and showers pushed the envelope for her. She absolutely refused to camp in state parks without those amenities.

Krista and Joel shared a problem that many couples have. The wife says she loves her husband just as he is, but then proceeds to recreate him into her desired image. How can couples like Krista and Joel bring truth into this arena?

Living the Truth

If you truly mean it when you say you love your husband just as he is, then the following three principles can help both of you live in that truth.

LOVE YOUR HUSBAND UNCONDITIONALLY

We all celebrate the fact that God loves us just as we are. Although he knows all our flaws, sins, and weaknesses, God still cares for us. (See 1 Peter 5:7.) We can't do anything to increase his love for us; we can't do anything to decrease his love for us. We embrace passages such as John 3:16–17: "For God so loved the world that he gave his one and only Son, that whoever believes in him shall not perish but have eternal life. For God did not send his Son into the world to condemn the world, but to save the world through him."

God could easily condemn us, but instead he showered us with undeserved love by sending his Son to take our place and provide us salvation from sin and death. Passages such as Romans 5:8 directly connect our sinfulness with God's unconditional love: "But God demonstrates his own love for us in this: While we were still sinners, Christ died for us."

Love means acting in the best interests of those we love. We bless them, we do good to them, and we make life easier and more fulfilling for them. In both of the above passages, God loved, and then he demonstrated that love by what he did. He didn't do that for us because we had treated him so well or done exactly what he wanted. He just loved. Period. He acted to benefit us. Period.

But we all know that, don't we? We need to move beyond simply knowing and into understanding that God's love for his people provides a pattern for how his people are to love one another, particularly for how husbands and wives are to love each other. The Old Testament book of Hosea describes how God told Hosea to continue to love his unfaithful wife, which provides a picture of God's love for us. Take some time to read through it; it won't take long. And as you read, remember the link between God's love for people and the marriage relationship.

In the New Testament, Paul affirmed that connection in Ephesians 5:23-25: "For the husband is the head of the wife as Christ is the head of the church, his body, of which he is the Savior. Now as the church submits to Christ, so also wives should submit to their husbands in everything. Husbands, love your wives, just as Christ loved the church and gave himself up for her."

Then, knowing that his readers might struggle to understand what he had just taught, Paul summarized it in verses 32-33: "This is a profound mystery—but I am talking about Christ and the church. However, each one of you also must love his wife as he loves himself, and the wife must respect her husband." Again we see a very clear linkage between the way God acts out of love for us and how we as spouses should act toward one another.

Wife, we don't intend to pick on you here, honest. Both husbands and wives need to love unconditionally, and the husbands got that message in our companion book, *Twelve Lies Husbands Tell Their Wives*. We're not letting them off easy. We just want to remind you that when you love your husband unconditionally, you are loving the way God loves. And that is a pretty good thing to do.

This concept of unconditional love provides the foundation for every other way to live in the truth. It means we don't look for reasons to avoid acting in love. Instead we act in love. Even when those we love don't deserve it. Even when they don't do what we desire. Even when we wish they were different. Even when we just don't feel like loving. We don't put conditions on doing the right thing. That leads us to understand acceptance.

ACCEPT YOUR HUSBAND

At its core, acceptance means receiving people as they are, for who they are, without requiring them to become something they aren't. Just as God accepts us as we are, so we should accept others as they are. Paul expressed this concept in Romans 15:7: "Accept one another, then, just as Christ accepted you, in order to bring praise to God." God receives praise when we Christians accept one another in the same manner Christ accepts us.

Rather than viewing a prospective husband as some good raw material that you can really work with, view him as a finished product. Of course, he'll change over the years—sometimes for good, sometimes for bad. But decide that you're satisfied even if he never changes. If you can't accept him as he is, then don't marry him. (Now that's honesty!)

If you're already married to a "project," change your attitude. Tell God and your husband that you truly love him as he is. (Of course, don't say it if it isn't true. If you're really struggling to love your husband unconditionally, ask God to help you look for what attracted you to your spouse at the beginning of your relationship, and ask him to help you actively look for things to love about your husband.) When those behaviors or character qualities that you'd love to change arise, remind yourself, "I love him just the way he is." As you keep repeating that mantra to yourself, you'll begin to change your perspective. You'll discover that you do accept him more all the time, just as he is.

DON'T IGNORE HIS SINS

Accepting your husband doesn't mean ignoring any sinful behavior. And, he will sin; he's human. (Keep in mind, we're talking about sins, not quirks that irk you.) Just follow the biblical pattern when he fails. First, talk to him about it. "If your brother sins against you, go and show him his fault, just between the two of you. If he listens to you, you have won your brother over" (Matthew 18:15).

Since he's a fairly sincere Christian guy, let's assume he

acknowledges his misbehavior and asks you to forgive him. What happens next? You forgive him. And forgive him if he does it again. Yes, that's biblical too.

When Jesus taught about confrontation, Peter grappled with the concept of forgiving repeated sin and asked Jesus to clarify it for him. In Jewish tradition, a person was required to forgive an offender three times if he asked for forgiveness. After three times, vengeance and retribution could follow. Peter more than doubled the traditional number and probably felt proud of his graciousness. "Then Peter came to Jesus and asked, 'Lord, how many times shall I forgive my brother when he sins against me? Up to seven times?' Jesus answered, 'I tell you, not seven times, but seventy-seven times'" (Matthew 18:21–22).

At a minimum, forgiveness means not continuing to bring up the offense. If you truly forgive your husband, you won't try to punish him. You won't refuse to act in love toward him because of his bad behavior. Of course, just because the offense pops up in your mind doesn't mean you haven't forgiven him. Each time the offense comes to mind, thank God that you have once and for all forgiven your husband.

And if the sinful behavior continues? Your husband may acknowledge it and continue to do the same thing, or he may refuse to acknowledge it at all. What should you do then? First, continue to love. Do the right thing anyway, because God calls spouses to love their mates unconditionally.

Second, evaluate the severity of the offense. Perhaps you can live with it. If so, accept the behavior as within the boundaries you can deal with and don't continue to make an issue of it. Keep repeating 1 Peter 4:8: "Above all, love each other deeply, because love covers over a multitude of sins." If husbands had to be sinless for wives to accept them, no marriage would endure. In marriage, we need to accept one another despite some sins.

But perhaps you can't live with it. If the sin involves abuse or unfaithfulness, in no way do we encourage you to meekly accept it. Sinful choices have consequences, and wives can act in love—truly wanting the best for their husbands—and still let them know that the behavior is incompatible with an active relationship. If they don't, they merely enable sinful behavior. Letting husbands face the logical consequences of their decisions doesn't violate love.

The difficulty comes when the offense lands in between acceptable and abusive. You can't accept the behavior, but it doesn't justify ending the relationship either. Our advice? Act in love, pray a lot, and get godly counsel about the specific situation you are facing. Talk with your pastor or see an insightful Christian marriage counselor. Don't go into denial and refuse to deal with the situation. The quicker you deal with it, the better off you and your husband will be.

BUT ACCEPT HIS QUIRKS

Assuming we're not talking about sinful or abusive behavior, how are wives to live in the truth about those quirks of their husbands that really frustrate them? What should you do when you just know that if your husband did what you wanted, he'd become a much better person? Quirks are those things husbands regularly do that are not wrong but irritating. Accept those quirks, even the ones that really bother you. Change your perspective so they don't bother you as much. You can mention the behavior to your husband once, but then let it rest.

On the day we wrote this passage, I (Sheila) saw Tim about to leave the house dressed in a certain gray pullover. I just don't like that shirt, although he does. And, I've mentioned it before. I mentioned it again. Now, that didn't start a big argument, but I should have just let it go. I don't want him to feel nagged about such a small issue.

When your husband does something that bugs you, say to yourself, "I love him just the way he is. He's a partner, not a project." It may take some time to accept that truth, but you can do it! Realize that his quirks don't amount to an impeachable offense. Let your love cover his flaws. Don't nag him to change; don't even mention it!

Feel free to pray about it, though! Ask God to change that quirk, if he wants to. Just don't "play Holy Spirit" and try to convict your husband on that issue. Rather, let it become a genuine nonissue. Decide on contentment even if God doesn't change him. Then, take your attitude to a deeper dimension.

APPRECIATE HIS QUIRKS

Once you've begun to accept your husband in those areas that used to annoy you, take the next step and thank God for them. Honest, we really mean it. Here's why. First, it's biblical! Without fear of contradiction, we can say that God wants you to appreciate your husband's quirks. Check this out: "Give thanks *in all circumstances*, for this is God's will for you in Christ Jesus" (1 Thessalonians 5:18).

Second, thanking God for quirks changes your mind-set toward them. It frees you from the pressure of needing to see a change before fully expressing your love to your husband. It allows you to begin to see God's hand in the situation. After all, God himself placed some of those quirks in your husband to make him unique.

When Krista realized that many of the traits she most wanted Joel to change were the same ones that initially attracted her to him, she started to change her thinking. "Yes, he does some risky things, like rock climbing. But he also took a risk to get his MBA to advance his career. And he took on that difficult assignment here in town, which allowed us to meet in the first place. I guess that's just who he is. I liked those qualities before. I can appreciate them now as well."

With that resolve, Krista began to appreciate Joel for who he was. As she did so, she noticed a number of changes occur.

ENJOY THE CHANGES

As Krista nagged less and accepted more, Joel began to share more of his life and thoughts. The acceptance he felt from his wife encouraged him to reveal more of his inner self since he now felt safer. Krista never dreamed that nagging him less to talk would result in his talking more.

That increased transparency enhanced their relational

intimacy. Krista didn't realize that men typically withdraw when they feel criticized and unaccepted. At the same time, they usually rely on their wives to be their closest friend when they feel safe. So as Joel felt more secure, he opened up to his wife in a number of areas, which increased the number of topics they could talk about. That increased number of topics deepened their overall connection since they shared more in common.

He could talk about the rock climbing and not get criticized. And Krista discovered some interesting facets about it she'd never known. She never got adventurous enough to try it, but she did see the allure it held for Joel, and so she didn't resent his rock-climbing trips. She still worried, but the resentment ended.

And, most curious of all, Krista noticed that Joel did begin to change in some of those areas that had previously bothered her. Once she quit trying to change him, and focused instead on changing her attitudes toward him, he didn't feel pressured to change. He didn't have to get defensive. He could change out of love for her, not because she tried to control him. On that basis, he didn't mind making some of the changes she wanted him to make, like reducing the amount of time he spent with his guy friends. He began spending some of that time with Krista, and they both enjoyed it.

Krista discovered that she really did love Joel, just the way he was. And that's the truth.

Lie 2

I'll Always Respect You— as Long as You Deserve It

The Truth about Respect and Appreciation

Five years of marriage had taken its toll on Will and Jessie. They'd married partway through college, and just after graduation she became pregnant with their first child. Will held a good job for several years, then lost it in a company-wide downsizing. He bounced around for awhile, working in temporary positions.

Several times they had to relocate for jobs. He stayed at one for almost two years, then an economic slowdown hit, and all those with low seniority lost their jobs. That included Will.

For Will and Jessie, financial uncertainty, distance from their families, and continual change combined to bring their marriage to the breaking point. Fortunately, their church had a family counselor on staff.

They met with Scott, who surveyed their struggles and began his discussion of the situation by focusing on their relationship.

"Will, apart from job issues and living so far from your families, if you could change one thing about your marriage, what would it be?"

Will never hesitated. "I'd want Jessie to criticize me less, to support me more, to respect me, to look up to me."

Jessie's reply came equally fast. "Will, I'd respect you

more if you could just keep a job for awhile. I'd support you if you supported me the way you should. I'd look up to you if you deserved it."

Then Jessie turned to Scott and explained her viewpoint. "Scott, we've battled this problem from the beginning of our marriage. Will just hasn't done his part. He wants me to respect him, but he doesn't realize that respect is earned. I hate to compare, but my dad has worked at a regular job for the last thirty years. He's always provided well financially for his family. I just don't think Will has enough motivation to get ahead, to take care of us."

"Jessie, I know I struggle sometimes," Will responded. "But when you criticize me, that just makes it more difficult. I hear a lot about what I don't do to please you, but I rarely hear about anything I do that's right. I'm not a totally bad person. What's the old line, 'You catch more flies with honey than with vinegar'? All I've been getting lately is the vinegar!"

"You're not a fly, you're a man," Jessie retorted. "So why don't you start acting like one, quit whining, and do what you should? I'll always respect you—as long as you deserve it."

The Lie

Jessie believed that respect should be given when earned and that Will's inability to hold a good job evidenced something about him and his attitude toward her. She saw no need to affirm him when he didn't do what she thought he should. She didn't recognize the central masculine need for respect and admiration, apart from the traditional male role as head of the household and primary breadwinner.

The previous lie focused on wives accepting their husbands as they are. This lie moves a step beyond acceptance and gets into liking them for themselves, appreciating what they do, and expressing respect and admiration for who they are.

On the Receiving End

In *The Proper Care and Feeding of Husbands,* Dr. Laura Schlessinger stated,

The universal complaint of men who emailed my website with their opinions about *The Proper Care and Feeding of Husbands* was that their wives criticize, complain, nag, rarely compliment or express appreciation, are difficult to satisfy. ... These are not men who hate their wives or who were divorced; on the contrary, they are guys who love their wives and are trying to do whatever they can to please them. However, they are miserable and lonely.[1]

Schlessinger identified two matched issues: (1) men need respect, and (2) when their wives don't give it, the husbands suffer and so does the marriage. Let's address that first issue of respect.

RESPECT: MEN NEED IT

About twenty years ago, we lived on a sloping half-acre lot in Fallbrook, California. Spring typically produced a tall crop of the wild grasses that covered most of the land. We had a self-propelled lawn mower with large rear wheels, but it broke down just as the growth season began. I (Tim) finally got it running again, but just as a push mower, and by that time the grasses had grown to nearly two feet in height.

My mom came down to visit, and she and Sheila took off for a day of shopping while I tried to get the yard presentable. Did I resent their playing while I sweated? Just a little. The temperature climbed close to a hundred degrees, and pushing the large mower on the slope drained me so much I had to stop several times to recuperate. I celebrated the conclusion of the task by collapsing on a gazebo swing in our backyard with a tall glass of iced tea.

Soon afterward, Sheila and Mom returned, and the first words from Sheila were, "Tim, that yard looks gorgeous. I thought we made a wrong turn and ended up at a park."

Well, it did look nice, but not necessarily on the level of a park! I found myself swelling up inside, ready to go out and mow the lawn again just to hear appreciation like that one more time. Any lingering resentment disappeared, and my spirit soared with love for my wife. I'd take on any task for appreciation like that.

God wired men to need appreciation and respect. Didn't Dr. Laura touch on that very issue? Her entire book resonates with it. In his first video series, Dr. James Dobson proposed that men predominantly build self-worth from the bricks of what they do.[2] Appreciation, then, is the mortar that holds those bricks in place.

The Bible makes a pretty strong statement about respect. Ephesians 5 talks about the husband and wife mutually submitting to the core needs of the other, and summarizes in verse 33: "However, each one of you [husbands] also must love his wife as he loves himself, and *the wife must respect her husband.*"

But just what is meant by respect?

The Amplified Bible translation of this verse leaves no doubt: "… and let the wife see that she *respects* and *reverences* her husband [that she *notices* him, *regards* him, *honors* him, *prefers* him, *venerates,* and *esteems* him; and that she *defers* to him, *praises* him, and *loves* and *admires him exceedingly*]."

Those translators wanted to be certain we got the message on that one! Since you may be rolling your eyes at the thought of respecting and reverencing, venerating and admiring your husband "exceedingly," let's explore what respect isn't.

Generally, men don't want their wives to continually praise them for how great they are. A few deluded souls may, but most don't expect constant adoration. Men don't look for worship. Nor do they wish their wives to ignore their personal failings and problems. They don't desire to run from reality and be above correction. But as one of Schlessinger's men, Bill, wrote, "There is a difference between complaining and informing, between criticizing and reminding."[3]

So how do wives show respect and appreciation for their husbands? Very simply, wives show respect for their husbands when they express admiration for their good qualities. When they value them. When they focus more on their successes than their failures. When they show that they're glad to be married to them. When they express appreciation for what their husbands do. Men tend to be fairly easy to please, and a simple "attaboy" goes a long way toward pleasing them. Mark Twain, a happy husband, said he could live for two weeks on one good compliment.

Well-placed, well-timed compliments mean the world to husbands, and a lack of respect and appreciation brings grave consequences.

WHEN THEY DON'T GET IT

When wives focus on failings, as Jessie did, when they don't balance their concerns with appreciation, then their husbands grow discouraged, as Will did.

One respondent to our survey said his wife continually criticized him without expressing any appreciation. His feelings alternated between shame, guilt, anger, and sadness. Other respondents stated that they felt discouraged because although they tried to meet the needs of their wives, they didn't receive any appreciation for their efforts.

Another husband said, "My wife insists that I be sensitive to her needs, that I listen to her, and meet her needs as she desires. That's fair, and I try to do that. But when I tell her I need just a little respect and appreciation, she says I'm being a baby. Why is it okay for her to ignore my needs, but not for me to ignore hers? I don't feel like she's as committed to me as she wants me to be to her."

Typically, when husbands don't get their needs met, they decrease their efforts to meet the needs of their wives. They divest themselves emotionally from the relationship, hoping to cut their losses. One husband said, "You know, if I expect my wife to show appreciation for what I do, and she doesn't, then I get real discouraged. But if I don't expect anything, I don't get as disappointed. I don't like it, but I don't know of another way to deal with it."

Behind the Lie

So why do wives buy into the lie that they don't need to respect their husbands—unless they "deserve" it? In part, they sometimes don't understand how much their husbands need to be respected and appreciated. Since they don't recognize the importance, they don't express that respect and appreciation.

When Tim and I (Sheila) go out to dinner with a particular couple, at the end of the meal the wife always says to her husband, "Thank you, honey." She makes many meals for him, yet I'm impressed that she doesn't take this special time as her due. She thanks him to show respect and appreciation.

Please don't get us wrong. Both husbands and wives need respect and appreciation. But we suspect that the need for respect and appreciation is stronger with men than with women. As a result, many wives don't comprehend the depth of their husbands' need, and consequently they don't concern themselves with it—at least not to the extent the husbands desire and deserve.

We also suspect that many wives avoid complimenting their husbands because it can increase their vulnerability. If their needs aren't being met, if they don't feel secure in the relationship, they may fear that giving respect and appreciation gives their husbands a more important role in their lives than they feel comfortable with. Or perhaps they're afraid that if they compliment their husbands, the men will think everything is fine, and the wives will never get their needs met. So, out of a sense of self-protection, the wives hold back.

Part of their reasoning may also come from the image of men as strong, independent, and self-sufficient. Some wives just can't imagine their husbands needing anything this much. So, giving respect and appreciation can appear to be catering to their husbands' immaturity rather than responding to a genuine need.

Each wife who resists giving appreciation needs to explore the specific reasons in her life that cause her to withhold expressions of admiration from her husband. Taking time to think through them, pray about them, and then perhaps discuss them will enable the couple to live in more of the truth.

Living the Truth

We've already seen that husbands have a particular need for respect and appreciation, but let's deepen our understanding of what they're really looking for.

EXTEND RESPECT TO ALL

We stress that wives should respect their husbands, but we do so in the context that all Christians should give respect to all people. Everyone needs appreciation, and we followers of Jesus have been told to extend it to all: "Show respect for everyone. Love your Christian brothers and sisters. Fear God. Show respect for the king" (1 Peter 2:17 NLT).

We need a continual attitude of respect to all people—particularly those we disagree with, which can often include our spouses: "Always be prepared to give an answer to everyone who asks you to give the reason for the hope that you have. But do this with gentleness and respect, keeping a clear conscience, so that those who speak maliciously against your good behavior in Christ may be ashamed of their slander" (1 Peter 3:15-16).

We Christians have earned a reputation for being judgmental, harsh, and legalistic. Yes, let's stand for the truth without wavering, but let's respect the right of others to disagree. As husbands and wives practice this respect with one another, much emotional stress can be decreased.

But a question arises. Apart from obeying God, why should we give respect to others, particularly our spouses? May we suggest that it is because respect flows from two causes.

RESPECT IS EARNED

Part of respect does come as a result of respectable behavior. Husband, we're talking to you right now. Do what you should to form the foundation for receiving respect. In our research we found a great quote from June Plessel: "No man has ever been shot while doing the dishes."

Now, we won't step on any toes and say that you should do the dishes! But the point remains: doing good things is a good thing. And good things earn respect. Granted, doing good things won't guarantee respect, but doing bad things will pretty much guarantee a lack of respect.

God even bases the respect due him on what he does. In Isaiah 5:12, God described people who enjoy the blessings that he brings, but who don't show appreciation for what he has done: "They have harps and lyres at their banquets, tambourines and flutes and wine, but they have no regard for the deeds of the LORD, *no respect for the work of his hands.*"

God himself wants appreciation for what he's done. We can find other biblical examples, such as Cornelius. In Acts 10:22, emissaries to the apostle Peter told him, "We have come from Cornelius the centurion. He is a *righteous and God-fearing man,* who is *respected* by all the Jewish people." Notice that Cornelius had *earned* respect for his righteousness and fear of God.

Now, let's move from examples to a general principle for all believers. "Make it your ambition to lead a quiet life, to mind your own business and to work with your hands, just as we told you, so that your daily life may *win the respect* of outsiders and so that you will not be dependent on anybody" (1 Thessalonians 4:11–12).

Good living earns respect. Husband, you need to live a life worthy of respect. Don't demand it; earn it. Again, that won't guarantee that your wife will respect you, but it begins the process.

RESPECT IS BASED ON POSITION

This section applies to the wife, and you may have noticed we just came to a huge potential loophole. Yes, we should respect all people. But if respect must be earned, then we can always find enough flaws to avoiding respecting some people. "Sam, you don't do the dishes, so …" "Loren, you don't provide well enough, so …" And no husband will fully earn the respect of his wife. That just can't be done, since every husband shares that universal human trait of being somewhat less than perfect!

So, sometimes we give respect based on the position, not the perfection, of the recipient. Here's a good example. While in college, Tim thought about joining the Navy Air Reserve. After graduation, he would have entered active service as an officer. At a family gathering Tim talked with his uncle Don, who had spent more than twenty years in the Navy and was a chief petty officer. With the arrogance of youth, Tim razzed Don, saying, "Guess you'll have to salute your nephew, huh?"

Don took him down a peg with his reply: "I'd salute the uniform, not the person." Respect is sometimes given because of the position, not because the individual has earned it.

Again, we find ample biblical precedent for this idea. Jesus told the story of a landowner whose tenants wouldn't pay the rent. He sent servants, whom the tenants disregarded, beat, and killed. "Last of all, he sent his son to them. 'They will respect my son,' he said" (Matthew 21:37).

Although the tenants had shown no respect for the servants, the landowner thought they would give it to his son simply because of the son's position.

The apostle Peter extended this principle of respect based on position specifically to those who don't particularly deserve respect based on their actions. "Slaves, submit yourselves to your masters with *all respect*, not only to those who are good and considerate, but *also to those who are harsh*" (1 Peter 2:18).

A lack of respectable actions doesn't allow us to withhold respect. Ephesians 5:33, the primary verse on wives giving respect, seems to refer to position as well: "… and the wife must respect her husband." We don't see an exception there, such as "… and the wife must respect her husband *if* he loves her unselfishly," or "*if* he helps around the house or brings her flowers or gets a raise." Rather, the rule is, respect him because he's your husband.

Wife, we realize that expressing respect and admiration can be difficult at times. But central to healthy marriages is meeting the core needs of your mate. Besides, you committed to do so when you married him. Now, on a very practical level, let's see how you can give respect and appreciation.

JUST DO IT

Let's explore five basic steps in expressing respect.

1. Focus on the positive. When relationships don't go as we had hoped, when people don't live up to our expectations, we can easily grow frustrated and critical. Of course, no husband has ever done everything perfectly according to his wife, but wives sometimes become expert at seeing the negative and ignoring the positive.

One of our survey respondents had a longer-than-expected recovery from surgery, and he admittedly could have done a bit more during his convalescence. His wife's frustration grew until she said, "You never do anything around here to help." Did he do some things? Yes. Could he do everything he normally did? No. Did he not do some things he could have done? Yes. But she focused on the negatives, ignored the positives, and made the issue into an absolute.

He shared how her comments impacted him. "You know, if she had appreciated what I did do, I could have acknowledged that I didn't do some things. But it became an all-or-nothing issue, and neither of us would bend."

Wife, we encourage you to look for the good qualities and acts of your husband. This doesn't mean that you should ignore real issues, but you should strive to establish a balance. We think that's biblical, as we see in the words of the apostle Paul addressed to the early believers:

> And now, dear brothers and sisters, let me say one more thing as I close this letter. *Fix your thoughts* on what is true and honorable and right. Think about things that are pure and

lovely and admirable. Think about things that are excellent and *worthy of praise.* Keep putting into practice all you learned from me and heard from me and saw me doing, and the *God of peace* will be with you. (Philippians 4:8–9 NLT)

Peace in marriage comes when both partners focus on the positive qualities of the other rather than their failings and weaknesses. Reinforcing good behavior with appreciation works far more effectively than complaining about failings. So we suggest that you begin the process by looking for the good attributes of your spouse. To help you do so, we have adapted the next three steps from *5 Love Needs of Men and Women* by Dr. Gary and Barbara Rosberg.[4]

2. Focus on him. Wives have a lot on their plates. Most face a combination of jobs, kids, household tasks, church responsibilities, and friendships to maintain. But back in Genesis, right after God established a relationship with Adam, he established marriage. We believe the primary human relationship should be marriage. Before the kids. Before other friendships. Before jobs. Before household tasks. Before anything else.

Men face the temptation to let their jobs take pre-eminence, and wives face the temptation to let other relationships take precedence. Resist those tendencies. Wife, each day, spend some time focusing just on your husband. That lets him know that you value him and your marriage, that he plays a central role in your life. Men need that reassurance, and only you can provide it for your husband. Put aside all the distractions, all the other good things, and focus on him.

3. Listen actively. Men tend not to have a lot of close relationships, so their marriage becomes a key arena of their self-expression. You show respect to your husband when you pay attention as he talks and shares his life, struggles, and dreams. Sometimes you can just listen to him without evaluating; he may simply need a safe place to share things he may not even believe.

Realize that men often talk about their dreams, knowing that they'll rarely become reality. Tim loves the mountains, especially Colorado. In the past, we'd drive through a gorgeous valley, and he'd often say, "I could live here."

I (Sheila) would typically freak out, thinking he meant to move the next week and uproot us from family and friends. I felt that I had no control over the situation, and that feeling sparked some disagreements between us. Tim has learned to be more careful in what he says, but I've also learned to interpret those statements as dreams and not plans.

I've also learned to ask some clarifying questions, such as, "Are you dreaming or planning here?" And, if his thinking is going beyond a dream toward something he might seriously consider, a gentle reminder can help: "Remember, if God wants us to move here, he can lead both of us."

Listen actively by asking questions to clarify your husband's meaning and to probe beneath the surface: "How did you feel when your boss changed your duties at work?" You can also reword and reflect his statement back to him: "Do you mean that you won't be in charge of new product development anymore?"

Your focused listening expresses respect.

4. *Support him.* Let him know that you believe in him. Every husband needs his wife to cheer him on. Again, this doesn't mean that you have to follow your husband's every whim, but do acknowledge his dreams and goals. You don't even have to agree with all his ideas. But let him know that you're on his side and that you stand behind him.

An old marriage quip reads, "Behind every successful man stands a good woman." A modern humorist changed it to "Behind every successful man stands a surprised woman." We like the first. Don't let your husband's successes surprise you, and stand behind him in his failures.

5. *Tell him.* Sometimes, giving more respect begins with adjusting your attitudes about the importance of it. Once you've changed your thinking, keep going. Don't stop with silent praise, but shower your husband with verbal appreciation.

Tell him you still love his body. Mention his good qualities to others when he's around. Briefly, without overdoing it, thank him for the things he does for you and the family. "Thanks for taking out the trash." Yes, it's his job, but he just likes to have his work noticed.

As you show respect and appreciation, you'll see a change in your husband. In Schlessinger's book, Janetta said, "I think men need respect—and the more respect they're shown, the more love they give in return."

We think she's right. Respect your husband, show your appreciation, and you'll benefit as well. And that's the truth.

Lie 3

I'll Love You for Richer or for Poorer

The Truth about Financial Partnership

In July of 2004, Senator John McCain of Arizona appeared on television with popular talk-show host Jay Leno. Someone had stolen his wife's credit card and spent a large amount of money. McCain addressed the anonymous thief over the airwaves. "All I want to say is thank you, and God bless you. You spent far less than my wife would have."

McCain touched on an area that may cause more dishonesty and conflict than anything else in marriage: finances. Most marriage counselors we've talked to suggest that money either lies at the heart of most conflicts, or is the primary expression of control issues.

In regard to finances, we've found two main arenas of friction.

Jamie and Teresa got ready for the annual office Christmas party, and when Teresa walked out of the bedroom, Jamie was just stunned. "Teresa, you look gorgeous in that dress. Did you just buy it?"

She seemed a little flustered at his comments and replied, "Thanks for noticing it! Yeah, I did just buy it. I got it on sale at Kohl's and only paid thirty-five dollars. Can you believe that deal?"

A few days later she met her cousin Peggy for coffee.

"Peggy, I almost got busted! Jamie *never* notices my clothes—new, old, or worn out. He's a guy! Then when I wore that new dress that I bought last week at Nordstrom, he asked if it was new. I was so shocked I almost couldn't talk. Imagine me not being able to talk! I blurted out something about getting it on sale at Kohl's, and he believed it.

"But I blew the clothing budget big time; that dress cost over two hundred dollars! I just couldn't tell him."

Before we began writing this book, we asked various women to give us the "lies" they tell most often. The topic of spending money and hiding it came up far more often than any other. One wife couldn't directly lie, so she'd buy a new dress, hang it in the closet for months without wearing it, then when she put it on, if her husband asked if it was new, she could truthfully say, "No, it's been hanging in the closet for months." Another wife opened a secret credit account to hide her purchases; the husband only discovered it when their credit report showed an unpaid bill on that account.

But some lies go much deeper. Like nearly every wife, Lori vowed to love Chuck "for richer or for poorer." She had come from a wealthy family, as had he, and she didn't anticipate any decrease in lifestyle. He made pretty good money as an investment adviser; she didn't have to deny herself too many desires. They had a nice home, car, and clothing. They traveled on vacations, staying at luxury resorts. And she kept her pledge until the "poorer" came along.

The recession of the early 1990s hit them hard. Chuck lost several accounts, and those that remained decreased in size and return. The couple had to downsize on their home, but since they'd bought at the market's high point, they still lost nearly a hundred thousand dollars. A Ford and a Dodge replaced their matching BMWs, and Lori began shopping at discount stores.

Even that decrease in expenditures didn't bring their lifestyle in line with their income, so Chuck said they'd have to find more ways to cut down on expenses. Well, that news pushed Lori over the edge.

"Chuck, I didn't sign up for this. This is not where I came from. This is not where I thought we were heading. I expected you to provide for my needs better. A lot of my friends are still doing okay; they don't have to cut down like we are. Their husbands take good care of them. I'm beginning to wonder about your commitment to me, about your ambition, about your ability. I just don't know why you're not supporting me in the way I know you can."

The Lie

Both of our stories reveal different dimensions of how wives can tell less than the truth about financial matters. Like Teresa, some wives hide their spending. They minimize the price they paid for new purchases or pretend that they aren't really new. Like Lori, some wives struggle to support their husbands in the latter part of the "for richer or for poorer" vows. Some time ago, we read of a study that indicated that among couples in which the husband is unemployed for nine months or more, the divorce rate hits 75 percent. This marriage failure occurs despite the wives' wedding vow, "I'll love you for richer or for poorer."

Behind the Lie

Why do wives involve themselves in this type of untruth? We'd like to suggest two primary reasons.

SPENDING BRINGS BENEFITS

In no way do we suggest that women like to spend more than men; both genders grapple with this issue. But we're examining how a wife's love of spending can result in her trying to hide the extent of it. Several factors can contribute to a wife's desire to spend. For some women, buying clothing and jewelry makes them *feel more attractive*. Our culture stresses physical beauty to the extent that most women feel great pressure to look better and better all the time. Nicer dresses, nicer jewelry, and overall nicer "stuff" increases attractiveness.

Spending can also *influence self-worth*. Unfortunately,

our culture also places a high value on wealth. Having nice things makes us feel better about ourselves and our degree of success. About fifteen years ago, I (Tim) bought a used pickup truck for my side business as a painting contractor while we planted a new church. Although the truck ran great, it had a few dents and needed a paint job. I certainly felt better about myself while driving it *after* the work on it had been done! We all have to develop an awareness of how stuff increases our self-worth.

Last, buying and having *nice stuff is gratifying.* We all enjoy it. Only ten years old, our granddaughter Hannah has some definite preferences. She likes nice stuff and will compare various items to find just the right one. The right hermit crab, the right shirt, the right sunglasses. She picks and chooses what she thinks she'll most enjoy.

When we moved to Fallbrook, I (Sheila) left my job of fifteen years, so we had to tighten our belts. I have a need to shop—to look, to handle, and to make decisions. Garage sales became just the thing. I could use my creative and artistic sides. I would come home with a treasure and scrub it up or repair it or give it whatever it needed. This hard work satisfied my need to shop and get nice stuff. Many times at church I'd get compliments on what I'd purchased at a garage sale, and I felt very talented. But at the same time I wished I could just go to a nice store and buy what I needed.

No matter where women shop, however, if the amounts haven't been mutually agreed upon, conflict can arise if their husbands find out. So, some wives spend to get the benefits and hide it to avoid the conflict. One of our survey respondents told why she hid the truth about some spending: "... so my husband wouldn't think I squandered our money, or to keep him from getting upset at my spending. ... It would only bring friction between us."

SPENDING BUILDS SECURITY

Wives usually have a higher need for security than most husbands, which can lead to attitudes toward money like the one Lori had. She resented Chuck because he didn't take care of her financial needs in the way she desired. God created us as material beings with material needs. He recognizes our need for housing, clothing, and food, a subject that we'll explore later in the chapter. In our culture, however, money provides these necessities.

So, concerns about a regular supply of money can threaten a wife's sense of security. And when threatened, many wives react with anger, attacks, and even hostility. Restrictions on spending can directly impact a wife's sense of security. When Tim quit pastoring in Fallbrook without having another job, I (Sheila) was not a happy camper. I had to go out looking for a job, and I felt resentful and angry about it. We then started a church in the nearby town of Temecula, where Tim worked as a painting contractor, but the irregular income brought me even more anxiety. This change in our financial situation took a real toll on our relationship, and I really only resolved it as I learned to trust more in God.

On the Receiving End

Husbands typically respond differently to untruths, based on which type of untruth they experience.

HIDDEN SPENDING

When wives hide their spending, the husbands have several responses. If the spending exceeds budgeted or agreed-upon spending limits, they view it as unfair. The family finances are stressed, and the husbands become resentful.

The degree of stress and resentment depends on the specifics. A one-time occurrence generally won't generate great problems. But repeatedly hiding spending increases the stress and can impact the relationship itself. One husband responded, "If she [the wife] has done it often, and he [the husband] finds out about it, [she] loses her credibility, and he always questions her honesty."

Another husband said he felt betrayed and wondered what else his wife had hidden from him.

So, the result moves beyond the actual money spent to relationship issues of trust. In trying to avoid some of the negative consequences of their spending, wives may bring even more significant consequences to the marriage. Those consequences can be greater when the money issue deals with the wedding vows.

FOR RICHER OR FOR POORER

God provided marriage as the closest relationship possible between a man and a woman. When it works right, marriage builds intimacy and unity, and provides a safe haven for both partners. And when it is done properly, marriage provides partners their best chance to love unconditionally as God does. That's why their marriage vows express a couple's intent to love beyond their circumstances: "for richer or for poorer; for better or for worse; in sickness and in health."

We recently saw the movie *The Notebook*, which wove together the younger and older lives of a couple. In the later years, the husband, played by James Garner, moved into a convalescent home to be with his wife, played by Gena Rowlands, who suffered from Alzheimer's. Their children tried to get him to come back home since she didn't recognize him. But his commitment to "for better or for worse, in sickness and in health" kept him with her in the home. To help her reclaim some of her memory, he often read her the story of their early days. What a marvelous example of unconditional love.

In cases like Chuck and Lori's, the husbands can view behavior like Lori's as a betrayal of their wedding vows. Chuck did. "Lori, when we did well financially, you thought I was the greatest guy on earth. You said that a lot. I haven't changed; I'm the same person. I work just as hard and just as smart as I did before. The only difference is our income. And now I wonder if you loved me at all, or just the money I brought in. What happened to your vows 'for richer or for poorer'?"

As we discussed in the last chapter, men need respect, appreciation, and support from their wives. When they put in a good effort to provide for the family, they've earned the right to be recognized as good providers. If they don't provide through their lack of efforts, that is a different situation, which we'll address a little later.

Criticism and lack of support on the level that Lori gave strike directly at the heart of husbands. Resentment grows, they withdraw from the relationship, and intimacy decreases. Yes, friction about money issues can threaten the very core of a marriage. How can couples deal with this crucial issue?

Living the Truth

Because each marriage has unique characteristics, how each couple lives in truth will vary. However, every couple can use these next two general principles to guide them into a greater level of truth in finances.

COMMIT TO THE PARTNERSHIP

We've built this book on the premise that our relationship with God comes first, our marriage comes second, followed by children and family, church, work, and then other issues. So, we need to have God's view on the importance of our marriage partnership.

First, according to Genesis 2:18, we need that partnership: "The LORD God said, 'It is not good for the man to be alone. I will make a helper suitable for him.'" Maggie Gallagher and Linda Waite researched the benefits of marriage in their book *The Case for Marriage.*[1] Allow us to summarize ten benefits of marriage, listed in reverse order.

> 10. *It's safer.* Bachelors experience violent crime four times more frequently than husbands.

> 9. *It can save your life.* Married men live ten years longer than single men.

8. *It can save your kid's life*. A parent's divorce decreases a child's life expectancy by four years.

7. *You earn more money.* After factoring in variables like college education and job history, married men typically make 40 percent more than bachelors.

6. *You get richer*. The average married couple at retirement has assets of about $410,000, versus $167,000 for the never married and $154,000 for divorced men.

5. *You experience greater faithfulness.* Men who live with a woman cheat four times as often as husbands; women who live with a man cheat eight times more often than wives.

4. *It's healthier mentally*. Married men are less depressed, anxious, and distressed than single men.

3. *It makes you happier.* Forty percent of married people describe themselves as "very happy," while only 25 percent of singles do so.

2. *Your kids will love you more.* Adult children of divorce see both of their parents less and describe less positive relationships than those whose parents remain married.

1. *You enjoy better sex.* Married people have sex more frequently than singles and report more satisfying sex lives.

Next, intimacy and transparency lie at the heart of marriage. A few verses later in Genesis 2 we read, "The man said, 'This is now bone of my bones and flesh of my flesh; she shall be called "woman," for she was taken out of man.' For this reason a man will leave his father and mother and be united to his wife, and they will become one flesh. The man and his wife were both naked, and they felt no shame" (vv. 23–25).

Partnership certainly includes the financial dimension. In contrast to some who believe the husband should be the sole financial provider, notice how, in Proverbs 31, the wife also contributes to the financial health of the family: "A wife of noble character who can find? She is worth far more than rubies. ... She considers a field and buys it; out of her earnings she plants a vineyard. ... She sees that her trading is profitable, and her lamp does not go out at night. ... She makes linen garments and sells them, and supplies the merchants with sashes" (vv. 10, 16, 18, 24).

To summarize, God gave us marriage as a partnership between a man and a woman. That partnership should benefit both parties, it should have transparency, and both husband and wife should make contributions to their financial health. Obviously, in such a relationship, honesty about financial matters and mutual support play vital roles.

However, both spouses face issues that work against this ideal type of partnership. First, God created men and women with significant differences. As we've noted, wives tend to value security, and husbands need appreciation. As males and females, our basic needs differ. Our communication styles differ. Our brains process information differently.

These differences are exaggerated by an innate human trait that both husbands and wives share: we want our own way. James said it well: "What causes fights and quarrels among you? Don't they come from your desires that battle within you? You want something but don't get it. You kill and covet, but you cannot have what you want. You quarrel and fight" (James 4:1–2).

Wives tend to focus on their own needs; husbands tend to focus on their own needs. Too often, both put their personal needs above the marriage and above meeting the needs of their spouse. So, we begin our first step toward living in financial honesty by valuing a transparent marriage that has financial health. We commit to living out our vows of "for richer or for poorer." Then we get practical.

CRAFT YOUR UNIQUE STRATEGY

Because every couple loves differently, each couple will need to build a strategy for financial transparency that flows from the dynamics of their marriage. We think these six steps can help you craft a plan for financial togetherness.

Speak the truth. Start with a commitment not to hide spending, to speak the truth, as Paul described in Ephesians 4:15: "Instead, speaking the truth in love, we will in all things grow up into him who is the Head, that is, Christ." In our survey, several wives said they should have been up front in the beginning. One wife said, "I delayed telling my husband for several days because I knew I shouldn't have bought it [a quilt] without discussing it with him first. Would he have said no if I had? Probably not. It was a stupid thing to do."

Honesty cuts in both directions. Wife, be truthful about your spending, about what is new and what isn't. We've seen some of the consequences that occur when wives are not totally honest. And husband, be honest about the family's financial condition. Don't exaggerate it to make yourself look better. Don't make it look worse to try to discourage your wife from spending.

Work together. Exactly how each couple works together will vary, but we encourage you to strive to live out the oneness described in Genesis 2:23–25. When I (Tim) do premarital counseling, I give the couples a one-question home-work assignment: "In practical terms, how can you best express oneness?"

Apply that question to your finances. Determine your spending patterns: Is one of you a careful saver? Are you both extravagant spenders? What are your financial goals? What arrangements have you made for savings? Retirement?

Vacations? Unexpected expenses? Some couples can't operate without a detailed budget. Others prefer to use only general guidelines. Which works best in your marriage?

Beyond basic expenses, we recommend that couples have individual "slush funds," money that each can spend without accounting to the other. Take it out of the family finances during each financial period—once a week, once a month, whatever works for you. This money shouldn't be spent on regular expenses; those should come out of the budget. But if either wants to go beyond budgeted amounts, the slush fund is available.

Wife, craft contentment. The wife can more easily exercise restraint in spending when that intimate partnership functions in a healthy manner, and when husband and wife work together. But whatever the circumstances, restraint is needed. Paul suggested that crafting contentment provides the foundation for that restraint.

> But godliness with contentment is great gain. For we brought nothing into the world, and we can take nothing out of it. *But if we have food and clothing, we will be content* with that. People who want to get rich fall into temptation and a trap and into many foolish and harmful desires that plunge men into ruin and destruction. For the love of money is a root of all kinds of evil. Some people, eager for money, have wandered from the faith and pierced themselves with many griefs. (1 Timothy 6:6–10)

We all can easily fall prey to the seduction of stuff—the desire for nicer stuff, more stuff. We deal with that temptation by choosing to be content with having our basic needs met. If we can have more, great. But if we never get beyond the basics, we still choose to be content.

A wife can express one other dimension of contentment. As we've discussed, our culture places great emphasis on physical beauty and resisting the ravages of aging. Those come with a high financial price tag. We certainly don't encourage you to ignore your appearance, but maybe the focus can be shifted to a more long-term perspective: developing character and faith.

Here is God's perspective as expressed by the apostle Peter:

> Your beauty should not come from outward adornment, such as braided hair and the wearing of gold jewelry and fine clothes. Instead, it should be that of your inner self, the unfading beauty of a gentle and quiet spirit, which is of great worth in God's sight. For this is the way the holy women of the past who put their hope in God used to make themselves beautiful. (1 Peter 3:3–5)

Peter didn't tell women to avoid looking good, otherwise a literal reading would require women not to wear clothing. Rather, he encouraged women to focus more on developing their spiritual beauty. Not all women can afford the financial costs of physical attractiveness, but all can develop spiritual beauty.

Wife, express support and appreciation. Let's assume your husband provides for the basic needs of the family, but not at the level you'd prefer. Assuming he makes a good effort, support him and express appreciation for what he does. Didn't you pledge to do so in your wedding vows? Also, as we discussed in the last chapter, realize that men have a deep need for respect and appreciation, and they usually respond better to affirmation than criticism.

Making our marriages work takes second place only to our walk with God. Having a healthy relationship should be more important than having nicer stuff. We encourage you to intentionally decrease your desires for spending money and acquiring stuff in order to improve your marriage. Don't let your husband think that you value things more than you value him.

Husband, provide for your family. Don't expect your

wife to restrain her spending if you don't do your best to provide for the family. Don't expect her to express appreciation and support if you don't do your part. When it's working right, marriage involves both partners submitting to the other, each placing the other above self. Don't ask your wife to do what you won't do.

Paul laid out the spiritual implications of this principle in 1 Timothy 5:8: "If anyone does not provide for his relatives, and especially for his immediate family, he has denied the faith and is worse than an unbeliever." That sounds serious to us, and we believe that many of the issues we've talked about would improve if husbands diligently provided for their families.

You don't have to work three jobs with no time for leisure and relaxation. You don't have to pull down a six-figure income. But provide for the basic housing, food, and clothing needs of your family. Be diligent. Work hard. Work smart.

Husband, be generous to your wife. Many husbands work hard, have a good income, and don't hesitate to spend money on themselves, but they begrudge anything their wives spend above the basics. We don't encourage financial irresponsibility, but we do encourage husbands to have a generous spirit toward their wives and their spending. Don't be a cheapskate. Though it probably goes without saying, stay within your income and budget.

God encourages generosity also. This next verse directly applies to giving to God, but in our opinion, it has a broader application: "Remember this: Whoever sows sparingly will also reap sparingly, and whoever sows generously will also reap generously" (2 Corinthians 9:6).

Once again, the specifics of generosity will vary in each marriage, based on the economic situation. But look for reasons to express generosity, rather than reasons to be stingy.

Why? We think you'll benefit. When the husband sets the stage for generosity, the wife is much more likely to respond by being honest about her spending. Husband, being generous may be the best thing you can do for yourself! And that's the truth.

Lie 4

You Aren't My Boss

The Truth about Submission

Helen Reddy's old song with the line "I am woman, hear me roar" could have used Tami as the model. Fiercely independent, she set her own course through life. She listened to the advice given by others, genuinely considered it, and then made her own decisions. Friends learned that they might convince her, but they could never push her into anything.

That independence and open mind combined to lead Tami to Christ. She met some Christians at the university she attended and went with them to hear a speaker. He talked about the historical roots of Christianity, the logic of its belief system, and the relationship offered by God through it. She talked to her parents, who never thought much about God and pretty much ignored him. She talked to her Christian friends about their experiences.

The truth of Christianity attracted her, but she struggled with yielding her will. The concept of letting another tell her what was best grated on her. Yes, it made sense if God was God, but she didn't particularly like it. But her keen mind realized that submission lay at the very heart of faith, and after several months of pondering, she made the commitment.

She got involved with a small group of students who studied the Bible together, and there she met James. He had grown up in church, wandered away from God during his first couple of years in college, and had started moving back. Their friendship grew, each providing a unique slant on faith that the other found refreshing. Romance blossomed, and two weeks after graduation, they married.

Tami began working at the preschool at their church and found she loved interacting with the children. They looked on her as just a bigger kid, and she enjoyed telling them the stories about Jesus that she herself had just discovered. James worked as a checker at the local supermarket while he looked for a permanent position in the computer programming field. But the technology bubble had just burst, and he found few options.

Then a friend who'd graduated a year before called and said his company had an opening that matched James' skills, and it offered a decent starting salary and benefits. The job, though, was several states away and would require relocation.

"Tami, I got some great news today. Remember Steve? He's working with that start-up in Washington, and they have an opening. It looks really promising. This has to be a God thing; it just fell into our laps. God is so good!"

"This is good? James, we'd have to move. And I just love working with these kids; I'm touching their lives, helping them explore the world, introducing them to the Bible. And you'd take that away from me? I don't know that I'd thank God for this one. It looks pretty bad from my perspective."

"Yes, I know we'd have to move. But sometimes we have to do things that we don't like. Career-wise, this is crucial for me. And the job pays enough so that you could quit working, and we could have some kids. This is a great opportunity for us as a family."

"So who made you the sole decision maker in our marriage? I thought this was an equal partnership. Don't tell me what's best for us without even asking me. You aren't my boss."

The Lie

Did Tami lie when she said, "You aren't my boss"? No, she spoke the truth. But along with rejecting the idea of "boss," she also dismissed the concept of submission. Yes, the pastor had talked about it in one of his sermons on marriage, but she rejected it out of hand as irrelevant in today's culture. She thought of marriage as an equal partnership: each party brought individual ideas, and they tried to come to a mutually agreeable decision. And if they couldn't agree, they wouldn't do anything. Neither husband nor wife had a more prominent or authoritative role than the other. Both should present their case with logic and firmness. The rights and opinions of neither partner should be trampled on.

Too often, we confuse submission with subservience. Let's explore the truth.

Behind the Lie

Why did Tami react so strongly? And why do so many men and women alike struggle with the concept of submission? We'd like to suggest two primary reasons.

SUBMISSION CONTRADICTS OUR CULTURE'S VALUE OF INDIVIDUALISM

Many today view submission as an alien concept, one that goes against all the values we cherish. America has a strong individualistic orientation in which persons take preeminence over communities. We stand up for ourselves and our personal rights. Because we all want to get ahead in life, often we place our needs above those of others, our wants and desires above our responsibilities and commitments.

Sports fans had a field day discussing the events of the free-agent signing days for the NBA in 2004. The Cleveland Cavaliers had a contract option for Carlos Boozer at seven hundred thousand dollars for the next year, and after that he would become a free agent. According to some, the Cavaliers had a handshake agreement with Boozer not to exercise the option so they could sign him to a new multiyear contract for forty-one million dollars. A nice increase. But, once he was released from the contract option, Boozer signed with the Utah Jazz for twenty-seven million more than his previous agreement.

What values cause such faithless, self-centered behavior? Materialistic values based on extreme individualism. Even former Cleveland teammate LeBron James, although hating to see Carlos leave, understood Boozer's action. "I told him he has to do what's best for his family." Forty-one million wasn't enough for his family? Without ever touching the principal, his income would have amounted to more than five hundred thousand dollars per year for eighty years. Most American families would gratefully accept that kind of salary.

And although America seems to typify this grasping for the most and the best of everything, human nature empowers it. James 4:1–2 reads, "What causes fights and quarrels among you? Don't they come from your desires that battle within you? You want something but don't get it. You kill and covet, but you cannot have what you want. You quarrel and fight."

When this thinking enters a marriage, the relationship becomes a duel of competing desires. We think our needs and our mate's needs are mutually exclusive, that there's no way to meet both. So we fight for ours. We stand up for ourselves. We determine that to submit is to show weakness and vulnerability, which, of course, we will not do.

SUBMISSION CONTRADICTS OUR CULTURE'S CONCEPT OF EGALITARIAN MARRIAGE

The second reason we struggle with submission has to do with a shift in marriage roles. During World War II, because so many able-bodied men were off fighting, many women took factory jobs. Harriet the Housewife transitioned into Rosie the Riveter, and the process of change began. After the war, and into the fifties, marriages reverted to the typical older pattern of the husband being the head of the household and the wife being the homemaker. But the change that started in the forties exploded in the sixties and seventies, and along with it, housing costs began to skyrocket.

Clearly, economics have driven part of the change in marriage roles. In many metropolitan areas, both spouses have to work simply to afford a mortgage. A recent study by the California Association of Realtors revealed that just 11 percent of households can afford to purchase a median-priced home in San Diego County. To purchase that home, a family needs an income of more than $130,000, which in most cases requires that both husband and wife work. Unless the husband is someone like Carlos Boozer.

As wives now share equally in the financial burden, they expect an equal role in the marriage. Equal partnership has become the key identifying mark of modern marriage, not only because of economic pressures but because of cultural influences as well. Equal rights for all has rightly become a key societal value.

When submission is mentioned in a marriage context, as it was in the 1998 statement of the Southern Baptist Convention, a firestorm of protest results. A feminist author, Maxine Hanks, said, "This notion of women being submissive to male authority is terribly out of balance and it prevents these churches from evolving into the enlightened Christian ideal they claim."[1] On his website, www.americanwasteland.com, on February 23, 2000, D. Marty Lasley said, "Several thousand white Southern Baptist pastors and their precious, meek, graciously submissive Stepford wives enthusiastically voted to turn back the clock to those antebellum 'glory days' when white men ruled supremely over their women, children, servants and slaves because their Bibles told them so."

Many see submission as a relic of fundamentalism that has no place in modern society because it stands in opposition to an equal partnership.

So, when we combine these two cultural values of individualism and egalitarianism, we can understand why submission has developed a bad name today.

On the Receiving End

Christian husbands find themselves on the horns of a dilemma. They have two options and get stuck with either. Wives often complain that their husbands won't act as the spiritual leaders of the family. But when the men exert some leadership, they come up against opposition and criticism as the women complain that the men aren't valuing their wives' input. Husbands feel as though they can't win no matter what they do.

James truly thought his career change would be good for the family. He imagined himself and Tami becoming parents, and he knew that his salary increase would allow her to stay home with the children. They'd talked about it before and agreed on the general plan. In his mind, he wanted to lead the family in this issue, and the solution he had been offered made perfect sense. He didn't understand why Tami was so upset.

We've seen three central results in men when the couples can't agree on the meaning of leadership and submission.

CONFUSION

James realized he didn't have a clue as to what Tami expected in this area of leadership and submission. She'd made some statements in their couples' Bible study group that led him to think she liked the idea of the husband leading the family. "But when I tried it, she fought it. I feel like she wants me to lead if I lead where she wants to go. And if she doesn't want to do what I think we should, then I'm being selfish and inconsiderate. How can I win? I'm criticized if I do and criticized if I don't."

We've talked to many men who experience this confusion. They don't have a clear idea of what spiritual leadership is or of what their wives think it is. They suspect it's more than praying at mealtime and less than pastoring a church, but they don't know where in the middle it lands. So, they muddle along, aiming for a target they can't see.

SPIRITUAL PASSIVITY

That confusion and conflict can lead to the next result: spiritual passivity. They try it, they fail; they try again. Once more they fail. Then they wait a while before another attempt, and failure again follows. Finally, their lack of understanding spiritual leadership and their wives' lack of acceptance causes them to give up the endeavor.

As a result, they back off spiritually. Both in leading the family and personally. Why set themselves up for failure? They're competent on the job, but maybe they're just not cut out to get deep into this "God stuff." Besides, they'd rather hear their wives' occasional complaints about their lack of a heart for God than to have to deal with continual conflict in their marriage.

But some men react another way.

A BATTLE FOR PREEMINENCE

Maybe these men have a stronger warrior gene, maybe they were taught extreme headship when they were younger; who knows? But when their wives resist, that resistance only motivates them to try harder. They don't give up the fight; they increase it. They won't admit failure. And their marriages become a battle zone of dueling desires for dominance.

Sometimes, when the husband wins, his mate becomes a Stepford wife: quiet, unassuming, and emotionally stifled. She gives in to his assertion of power and loses her personhood in the process. In this situation, abuse—verbal, emotional, or physical—is common.

The dazed and confused husband, the spiritually passive husband, and the power-hungry warrior husband are not what God had in mind when he gave his pattern for marriage. What's the truth about submission?

Living the Truth

Perhaps submission confuses us because it's linked with headship, marriage, men and women, and human nature. We can't help but think of it as Winston Churchill described the

Soviet Union: "a riddle wrapped in a mystery inside an enigma."[2] So before we get into how submission relates to marriage, let's try to understand submission itself.

For starters, here's a working definition of *submission:* Submission is the mutual and voluntary lifting up the needs of others above our own. We'll expand on that definition as we go, but we want to look first at what happens when individuals choose not to submit.

WHEN SUBMISSION IS LACKING

When submission is lacking in a person's attitudes and behaviors, a wide variety of negative consequences result.

A hostile spiritual attitude. Submission begins with our relationship with God. If we won't submit to him, we can't connect with him. Romans 8:7 tells us, "The sinful mind is hostile to God. It does not submit to God's law, nor can it do so."

Submission stands in contrast to hostility. When we reject submission, whether with God or with a spouse, hostility will frequently result. Obviously, hostility can come from a variety of sources, but a lack of submission certainly is one.

Ineffective prayer. Most of us feel guilty about our prayer life and its lack of effectiveness. But Jesus demonstrated that submission to God opens up a dynamic prayer life. "During the days of Jesus' life on earth, he offered up prayers and petitions with loud cries and tears to the one who could save him from death, and he was heard because of his reverent submission" (Hebrews 5:7).

Even Jesus, the only Son of God, had his prayers heard because he submitted to the Father. So, perhaps, if our prayers bounce off the ceiling, we should evaluate our level of submission to God.

A rebellious attitude. Romans 13:1-2 extends submission to our attitudes toward the authorities in our lives. "Everyone must submit himself to the governing authorities, for there is no authority except that which God has established.

The authorities that exist have been established by God. Consequently, he who rebels against the authority is rebelling against what God has instituted, and those who do so will bring judgment on themselves."

Although the passage specifically refers to the government, it reveals something about our views toward any valid authority. When rebelliousness runs through us, submission departs.

A selfish spirit. In Ephesians 5:21–6:9 the apostle Paul provided the preeminent discourse on submission. In verse 21 he set the theme for the entire section: "Submit to one another out of reverence for Christ." He then told us how to submit in marriage, with children, and at work—with the most instruction on marriage. He summarized the concept in verse 33:"However, each one of you also must love his wife as he loves himself, and the wife must respect her husband." Or, to put that in our own words, we submit when we give up our selfish desires and commit to meet the needs of our spouse.

Male spiritual dominance. While the word *submission* doesn't appear in the following passage, the principle still applies. In Galatians 3:28 Paul gave a foundational understanding of the relationship between husbands and wives: "There is neither Jew nor Greek, slave nor free, male nor female, for you are all one in Christ Jesus."

A popular seminar leader champions the belief that husbands are the priests of the family. The role of a priest is to be a go-between, a bridge builder. In this view, the wife connects with God through her husband. But if male and female are one in Christ, then each connects directly with the Father through Jesus. Wives don't connect with God through their husbands; they can do that on their own.

Headship (covered in our companion book *Twelve Lies Husbands Tell Their Wives*) too often leads to "bossism" instead of spiritual leadership. Bossism doesn't find any support in Galatians 3:28.

Worldly attitudes. James 3:14–18 gives an extensive

listing of traits that contrast with submission. James put submission at the center of godly wisdom, which stands in opposition to worldly attitudes.

> But if you harbor *bitter envy and selfish ambition* in your hearts, do not boast about it or deny the truth. Such "wisdom" does not come down from heaven but is earthly, unspiritual, of the devil. For where you have envy and selfish ambition, there you find *disorder* and every *evil practice.* But the wisdom that comes from heaven is first of all pure; then peace-loving, considerate, *submissive,* full of mercy and good fruit, impartial and sincere. Peacemakers who sow in peace raise a harvest of righteousness.

Godly wisdom, centering on submission, won't exist along with envy, ambition, disorder, evil, and conflict.

A lack of spiritual beauty. We've noticed a number of people who, although not blessed with great physical attractiveness, seem to glow with an inner beauty. Others have beautiful features but don't appear attractive. The difference may be submission!

> Your beauty should not come from outward adornment, such as braided hair and the wearing of gold jewelry and fine clothes. Instead, it should be that of your inner self, the unfading beauty of a gentle and quiet spirit, which is of great worth in God's sight. For this is the way the holy women of the past who put their hope in God used to make themselves beautiful. They were submissive to their own husbands. (1 Peter 3:3–5)

We realize you won't find this prescription for beauty in the pages of supermarket tabloids or women's magazines, but, according to Peter, God himself associates beauty with submission.

A lack of concern for the husband's spirituality. If we go back a few verses in 1 Peter 3, we find another contrast to submission. Ironically, many wives wish their husbands would provide spiritual leadership, but their lack of submission prevents the fulfillment of their wish. "Wives, in the same way be submissive to your husbands so that, if any of them do not believe the word, they may be won over without words by the behavior of their wives, when they see the purity and reverence of your lives" (1 Peter 3:1–2).

Peter said that submissiveness can advance the spiritual journey of a wife.

Overall, every contrast to submission reveals something negative. Now, let's flip the coin and look more closely at submission.

WHO SUBMITS TO WHOM?

We discovered that submission involves much more than wives submitting to their husbands. We hope these passages will expand your understanding of the role of submission.

Jesus submitted to the Father. We covered this subject above, so let's just scan the verse again. Jesus doesn't ask anyone to do what he wouldn't do, and that includes submitting. "During the days of Jesus' life on earth, he offered up prayers and petitions with loud cries and tears to the one who could save him from death, and he was heard because of his reverent submission" (Hebrews 5:7).

We can't call submission an outdated concept if Jesus himself did it. Something good and holy is wrapped up in the concept.

Christians are to submit to God. Submission to the sovereignty, authority, and love of God stands at the center of the entire Christian life. We read a passage earlier that says that sinful minds cannot submit to God. People who want to follow Christ can, and should, submit to the Father. This verse comes just after an earlier passage that contrasts submission with having worldly attitudes. "Submit yourselves, then, to God" (James 4:7).

Submission is to be a characteristic of the typical Christian life. Jesus was submissive to his heavenly Father. And we can and should do the same thing. Now, let's move beyond submitting to God and explore how submission touches our relationships with each other.

Christians are to submit to one another. We also mentioned this one before, but we extracted another principle then. Now, let's get to the heart of it. We'll use the New King James Version here, because it best reflects the original grammar of Ephesians 5:18–21:

> Be filled with the Spirit, *speaking* to one another in psalms and hymns and spiritual songs, *singing* and making melody in your heart to the Lord, *giving thanks* always for all things to God the Father in the name of our Lord Jesus Christ, *submitting to one* another in the fear of God.

"Be filled" is the command, a general command for all Christians for all times. Then Paul gave four participles (the italicized words that end in "ing") that explain how to be filled. Later, Paul described how submission works between husbands and wives, parents and children, and employers and employees. But it all begins with a command to be filled. And we can't be filled with the Spirit without a willingness to submit to one another. This trait of submission shocked the world in the first century. Unbelievers saw Christians sacrificially helping one another, sharing their substance. Tertullian, a pagan Roman historian, commented, "Look at how they love one another." Why? The reality of their submission expressed itself in practical terms.

Please grab onto this concept. Submission isn't a burden inflicted on wives to force them to obey domineering husbands. Submission is a characteristic of the normal Christian life—for all Christians.

Church members are to submit to their spiritual leaders. Now we start to get specific on submission. No church can carry out its mission unless the leaders lead biblically and the followers follow authentic spiritual leadership. Notice the dual roles in Hebrews 13:17 (NKJV): "Obey those who rule over you, and *be submissive,* for they watch out for your souls, as those who *must give account.* Let them do so with joy and not with grief, for that would be unprofitable for you."

The Word of God says that joyful submission is profitable. It doesn't say, however, that church members must submit to autocratic, self-serving leadership. Leaders must give an account to God for how they lead, and the New Testament offers abundant instructions for how leaders are to lead for the benefit of the overall church. When the local church functions as it should, it cares for its members, it reaches the community, and it becomes a healthy part of the body of Christ.

On the flip side, if the members won't submit, leaders spend all their energy putting out brushfires. Again, submission is supposed to be the normal church life.

Christians are to submit to the government. This principle provides another slant to the one we just discussed. Just as churches can live in harmony and peace when their members submit to spiritual authority, so countries can live in peace when their citizens submit to political authority.

> Everyone must submit himself to the governing authorities, for there is no authority except that which God has established. The authorities that exist have been established by God. Consequently, he who rebels against the authority is rebelling against what God has instituted, and those who do so will bring judgment on themselves. For rulers hold no terror for those who do right, but for those who do wrong. Do you want to be free from fear of the one in authority? Then do what is right and he will commend you. (Romans 13:1–3)

Do you grasp the concept that submission flows through all we do as Christians? If so, then the next section will make perfect sense to you.

Wives are to submit to their husbands. As part of being filled with the Spirit, as part of all Christians submitting to one another, wives should submit to their husbands. Ephesians 5:21, the general command for all Christians, leads into verse 22: "Wives, submit to your husbands as to the Lord."

Lest we think that's all, we find the command repeated both in Colossians 3:18, "Wives, submit to your husbands, as is fitting in the Lord," and also in 1 Peter 3:1, "Wives, in the same way be submissive to your husbands."

It seems pretty clear that the Christian trait of being submissive applies to wives in regard to their husbands. Now, let's figure out just what it means to submit.

THE HEART OF CHRISTIAN SUBMISSION

We could sum up all we've covered so far by repeating the definition of *submission*: the mutual and voluntary lifting up the needs of others above our own. Remember, Jesus provided the pattern for us to submit, and we find a marvelous retelling of his actions in Philippians 2:1–7.

> If you have any encouragement from being united with Christ, if any comfort from his love, if any fellowship with the Spirit, if any tenderness and compassion, then make my joy complete by being like-minded, having the same love, being one in spirit and purpose. Do nothing out of selfish ambition or vain conceit, but in humility consider others better than yourselves. Each of you should look not only to your own interests, but also to the interests of others. Your attitude should be the same as that of Christ Jesus: Who, being in very nature God, did not consider equality with God something to be grasped, but made himself nothing, taking the very nature of a servant, being made in human likeness.

Just as Jesus submitted to the Father, he also submitted to our needs. And unity and effectiveness in the Christian community will come only when we sacrifice our desires and needs for the desires and needs of others. As Jesus did. That doesn't mean that we should ignore our needs, only that we shouldn't selfishly put our needs first, ahead of the needs of others.

Gale Sayers, the Hall of Fame running back for the Chicago Bears, told his secret to JOY: Jesus first, Others second, and Yourself last.

That sounds like the Christian life, doesn't it?

THE HEART OF SUBMISSION FOR WIVES

Husbands must never use their wives' submission as an excuse for male domination or bossism. There is no biblical command for husbands to tell their wives to submit. Husbands are told to sacrifice; that's their role. Wives are told to submit; that's their role. Jesus didn't pattern domination, but sacrifice. If done willingly and with the right attitude, that sacrifice by husbands rules out any imbalance in the marital relationship caused by their wives' submission.

Wifely submission doesn't include saying yes to ungodly requests by their husbands. We've heard Christian teachers tell wives to obey their husbands even if they want them to engage in sexual immorality. Wifely submission follows sacrifice by the husband. Submission doesn't diminish but enhances a wife's individuality. In the Ephesians 5 passage, Paul wrote that a husband should have the same goal for his wife that Christ has for the church: "to make her holy, cleansing her by the washing with water through the word, and to present her to himself as … radiant … without stain or wrinkle or any other blemish, but holy and blameless" (vv. 26–27). Husbands and wives should not fear that mutual submission will bring damage to either or both of them; rather they should be comforted that God designed it to enhance their shared life.

In their book *5 Love Needs of Men and Women,* Dr. Gary and Barbara Rosberg offer five suggestions for how wives can submit to their husbands and help them be the spiritual leaders in their marriages and families.[3] We've reworded those tips to apply to submission by the godly wife.

1. Don't play junior Holy Spirit. Since we each can access God directly, don't think that you have to point out every flaw you see in your husband. Yes, deal with issues that arise; let him know when he wrongs you. Submission doesn't include either of the extremes of putting up with sin or of pointing out every sin. Allow the Spirit to work on your husband and convict him of his wrongs.

2. Accept the risk of failure and imperfection. Wives often have high expectations of their husbands, and spiritual leadership does correspond with spiritual sensitivity and maturity. Failure to live up to these expectations breeds disappointment. Typically, frustration is experienced when reality doesn't match expectations, and the larger the gap, the greater the frustration. So when wives lower their expectations, they also lower their frustrations.

Ironically, husbands often resist change when they feel their wives are forcing them into it. Men don't like to be told what to do. So as wives back off and accept some imperfections, husbands often make changes once they can do so without seeming to cave in. Wife, that principle may not make sense to you, but your husband may be nodding his head as he reads it.

3. Pray for him. Prayer works, even if your husband doesn't see you praying. Pray thankfully for him. Pray blessings on his life. Pray that God will speak to him about the areas of his life he needs to change. Pray that you will become the wife he needs and desires you to be.

Praying for someone tends to soften our heart toward that person. Perhaps that's why Jesus told us to love our enemies and pray for those who abuse us (see Matthew 5:44). Sometimes, husbands fit into those categories, don't they? Prayer is a great way of acknowledging the needs of your husband and increasing your commitment to meet those needs.

4. Praise him. We covered this point in Lie 2, as we explored the truth about respect and appreciation. Let's not cover old ground, but do remember that husbands have a strong need to know that they are respected for who they are and appreciated for what they do. When your husband does something good, tell him. You don't have to go overboard and fawn all over him, but a discreet compliment works wonders on a husband. Particularly, when he has a spiritual victory, or when he takes a spiritual stand, your noticing and affirming it will reinforce that behavior.

5. *Be a spiritual helper.* In Genesis 2:18, God established the basic relationship between husband and wife. "It is not good for the man to be alone. I will make a *helper* suitable for him." *Helper* doesn't mean servant, but strength. In Psalm 118:6-7, the Bible calls God our helper. Because the man couldn't experience the abundant life on his own, God provided the woman to make up for what he lacked.

So, be on your husband's side spiritually. Encourage him. Work around his weaknesses. Maximize his strengths. Develop the goal of becoming a positive spiritual influence in his life.

Enjoy the Results

We truly believe that submission provides the foundation for healthy relationships across the spectrum—with God, church members, other Christians, and marriage partners. In submission we get beyond focusing on our needs and learn to look out for the needs of others. Maggie Gallagher contributed a chapter to the book *Does Christianity Teach Male Headship? The Equal-Regard Marriage and Its Critics.* In it, she refers to a finding by sociologist Brad Wilcox.

> Conservative Protestants, who are the only group of people actively advocating for male headship in our society and for a strong vision of gender difference, oddly enough turn out to produce husbands and fathers who are more like the "new man," that is, a warm, engaged, attentive father. And their wives report that these men are also more appreciative, *and the wives are happier* than the average wife or the wives of religiously unaffiliated men. This is true only for conservative Protestants who go to church. If you're a nominal conservative

Protestant and you just pick up on the headship ideology and you don't have the idea of
love and sacrifice for the sake of your family, it
turns out badly.[4]

Headship and submission work when done biblically.
Allow us to refer to the premier passage on that idea, Ephesians
5:21–33. Paul summarized godly submission in verses 32–33:
"This [headship and submission] is a profound mystery—but I
am talking about Christ and the church. However, each one of
you also must love his wife as he loves himself, and the wife
must respect her husband."

Husband, don't just look after your own needs. Sacrifice
them as Christ did. Take the lead in submitting to your wife's
need to be loved. Wife, you can relax and not stress over your
needs being met, and you can then submit to your husband's
need for respect and appreciation. He will then think, *What a
great wife; I love her so much.* You will then think, *What a
great husband; I love him so much.* And the two of you will
marvel and rejoice as your marriage just gets better and better.
And that's the truth.

Lie 5

I'll Never
Be Unfaithful to You

The Truth about Faithfulness

S uzie never planned the affair. Her marriage to Jack pretty much met her needs emotionally, physically, and spiritually. She had some frustrations about his busyness and the fact that he didn't talk much, but she could accept those things—she thought. Perhaps that thinking increased her vulnerability just enough, because she wasn't even worried.

She had no concerns about the working lunches with her boss. Their conversations focused on work issues, and only slowly did they begin to bring in personal issues. She appreciated how he listened and gave support without giving advice. He told her of his struggles with the company and his dreams for the future.

Along with a dozen coworkers, Suzie and her boss attended an out-of-state convention; they all met for a closing critique one night in his suite at the hotel. The others slowly drifted back to their rooms, except Suzie. She stayed all night.

Deena loved to watch soap operas; they fed her hunger for romance in a way that Derrick never did. He provided well, he loved God and his family, but he tended to be quiet. Not quite boring, just stable and solid. He was a rock, and she yearned for fire.

Mike, however, met all the standards of her ideal man. He

led the small Bible group they attended, and the twinkle never left his eyes. He ran his own business, rode a motorcycle, and had adventure written all over him.

Sometimes at the group meetings she'd imagine riding the motorcycle with him, her arms tightly wrapped around him, her head against his back. A few times while making love with Derrick she imagined Mike in Derrick's place with her, but she tried to minimize that kind of imagery. She knew it was just a fantasy; nothing like that would ever happen. Thinking of Mike as she did held no danger; she wanted to remain faithful to Derrick.

Shannon's full life left little room for her husband, Barry. She worked part time at the local fitness center as a personal trainer and volunteered several nights each week at a hotline for abused women. She team-taught a class for third-graders at church, which took another night each week for preparation. She got together with her girlfriends once a month for Bunco and met her mom one day each week for lunch.

Barry's frustration finally came to a head. "Shannon, I don't know why we got married; we spent more time together when we were dating. Our meals are rushed; you're hardly around. I feel like I'm just a paycheck to you. On your list of priorities, I feel like I come in after your work, your friends, your mom, and your fun. In the premarital counseling sessions, Pastor George talked about marriage as two becoming one. I'm barely even on your schedule. We don't have time to become one!"

Though their stories differ, Suzie, Deena, and Shannon share one common trait: unfaithfulness.

The Lie

Let's begin by defining *faithfulness* as living up to vows and promises. *Unfaithfulness*, then, involves not living up to vows on a significant or ongoing basis. *Adultery* occurs when there is a gross violation of marriage vows. That violation can take three different forms.

PHYSICAL ADULTERY

Most of us would acknowledge that a married person who becomes sexually involved with someone other than his or her spouse is committing adultery. God prohibited adultery in the Ten Commandments (see Exodus 20:14), and Jesus affirmed God's words in Matthew 5:27: "You have heard that it was said, 'Do not commit adultery.'"

Pretty clearly, this definition of adultery addresses the behavior of Suzie in our first story.

EMOTIONAL OR MENTAL ADULTERY

Jesus took adultery a step further in the next verse: "But I tell you that anyone who looks at a woman lustfully has already committed adultery with her in his heart" (Matthew 5:28).

Deena battled with this form of adultery. In her mind, she made love to Mike. She not only allowed the fantasies to run around in her head, she also invited them into her heart and played with them.

ADULTERY BY NEGLECT

Neglect may seem hard to acknowledge as adultery until it is recognized that adultery involves unfaithfulness to any of the marriage vows, not just the ones that cover sexual fidelity. In Jeremiah 9:2 the prophet clearly equated adultery with unfaithfulness: "Oh, that I had in the desert a lodging place for travelers, so that I might leave my people and go away from them; for they *are all adulterers, a crowd of unfaithful people.*" So, unfaithfulness equals adultery.

Let's move a step deeper here. In their marriage vows, couples promise to love one another. Faithfulness means they do; unfaithfulness means they don't. In Romans 13:9 the apostle Paul connected a lack of love to adultery: "The commandments, *'Do not commit adultery,' 'Do not murder,' 'Do not steal,' 'Do not covet,'* and whatever other commandment there may be, are summed up in this one rule: *'Love your neighbor as yourself.'*" Marriage partners cannot be faithful to their vows if they don't love their mate as they love themselves.

So, when wives vow to their husbands, "I'll always be faithful to you," and yet commit adultery in any of these three ways, they lie.

On the Receiving End

Husbands can experience a wide range of reactions to their wives' unfaithfulness, depending in large part on the relationship, the severity of the wives' actions, and the degree of the husbands' knowledge.

PHYSICAL ADULTERY

Jack never had a clue in the months leading up to Suzie's affair. He'd noticed her being a little more distant but thought it just came from work pressures. But when he found a note from her boss, he realized it wasn't work pressure but work pleasure that had caused the distance. That note devastated him.

He'd been scrupulously faithful and couldn't understand why she hadn't been. He couldn't imagine her sharing something as intimate as sex with another person. He had dreamed of spending his life with her—just her—but now he feared that their relationship could never go back to the innocence they'd once enjoyed. The oneness he'd cherished with her had disappeared.

Suzie wanted to work things out and save their marriage, but Jack wondered if they could. He questioned whether he really knew her, since he never thought she'd do something like this. He'd never experienced such deep pain and sense of loss, and he didn't know whether he could get over it.

EMOTIONAL OR MENTAL ADULTERY

Derrick never dreamed that Deena fantasized about Mike as she did. Yes, he saw her looking at Mike intently during the Bible studies, but after all, Mike led the discussion. And when the two of them talked, it just seemed like ordinary conversation to

Derrick. He remained pretty clueless. Until she asked him why he couldn't be more like Mike. He blew it off the first time, but when she did it a second time a few weeks later, he got a little irritated. Her expectations had always seemed unrealistic, as though she lived in a dream world with ideal people. He knew he couldn't live up to those standards. No one could, although she seemed to think Mike did. But he'd spent some time with Mike and knew the man had his flaws.

When Deena started mentioning Mike more often, Derrick began to wonder a little more. She seemed to grow more and more frustrated with Derrick, and he grew more frustrated with her comparing him to Mike. A wall grew between them, a wall they couldn't tear down. To Derrick, it seemed that Deena didn't want to do so.

ADULTERY BY NEGLECT

Barry felt ignored and unvalued by his wife, but he never would have called her behavior "adultery." When he tried to talk about it, Shannon called him a baby. After that he never brought it up again. Not one to sit around and sulk, he started to create his own life apart from Shannon. He joined a men's group at the church, played on the sports teams, and built a circle of guy friends.

He never contemplated divorce; he took the situation as part of "for better or for worse." And it definitely fit the "worse" category; so he resigned himself to an unhappy marriage, one that didn't come close to meeting his needs, but one that he'd stick out. Then he and Bob talked about it one day.

"Barry, I listen to that Dr. Laura show, and the other day some guy called in, and it could have been you. His wife didn't seem to care about meeting his needs, kinda like Shannon. He called it 'the moral equivalent of infidelity.' Man, that caught my attention. Then Dr. Laura agreed! She talked about how the vows include things like love, honor, protect, and care for. That maybe we could think of breaching any of those vows as infidelity. Anyway, it made me think."

"You know," Barry replied, "Shannon would accuse me of

not keeping my vows if I quit working and just lay around the house. And, I think she'd be right. But maybe that's a two-edged sword; it cuts both ways."

Barry didn't make plans to find an attorney and divorce Shannon, but he realized that she was breaking her vows and being unfaithful to him.

Behind the Lie

Why would Christian women like Suzie, Deena, and Shannon break their marriage vows? Multiple reasons exist, depending on the individuals and their backgrounds, the situations, their marriages, and the type of adultery.

Physical Adultery

Sex itself provides a strong motivation for sexual infidelity. Some may say this reason doesn't exist in Christian families, nor with women, but that view expresses naiveté. Some married Christians are sexually unfaithful to their mates, and some women commit adultery for the physical pleasure of sex. When Tim attended Sexaholics Anonymous meetings, the number of women there surprised him, and nearly all came from a church background.

Unmet emotional needs provide another cause. The husband may not meet his wife's emotional needs, or her needs may be so high that no husband could meet them. A deficit of emotional needs can create a great susceptibility for some women.

Unmet relational needs can do the same. When a woman's needs for connection, for feeling cherished and loved, aren't met, she can face great vulnerability when someone other than her husband pays her attention. She doesn't want the sex as much as the relationship, and sex becomes a means to that end.

Emotional or Mental Adultery

Some women feel very good that they don't act on their feelings of infidelity. Since they don't actually engage in physical adultery, they think they don't hurt anyone; they don't take anything that belongs to someone else. Since no one even knows what's going on, no one gets hurt. They believe what they're doing is okay, but they are ignoring Jesus' comment about adultery coming from the heart.

Each of the above factors can lead women into emotional adultery, but several others can also contribute.

A romantic, idealistic view of the world, like the one Deena had, can lead to fantasy affairs. Real life just can't match the world in their minds, so these women live an imaginary Cinderella existence.

Some view the safety of the fantasy world as a huge benefit. Since there is no risk of pregnancy, abortion, divorce, AIDS or other sexually transmitted diseases, they think they have eliminated the risks and vulnerability of real relationships. Since no one knows about them or is harmed by them, they think these fantasy affairs are safe from God's judgment. Also, since they are private and secret, they think that by engaging in them they can hide from life. Life may be a disappointment to them, and they may view themselves as losers—except in their fantasy world. Their "dream lovers" never have bed hair or morning mouth. Their dream men never get short with them, never come home late, never forget their birthday, never fail to show them tender loving care. On the contrary, they are always perfect gentlemen, immaculately groomed, attentive to their every wish and desire—continually showering them with lovely compliments, beautiful flowers, and expensive gifts for no reason at all, except that they simply adore them. Quite a fantasy, indeed!

ADULTERY BY NEGLECT

Three primary reasons lead to neglectful adultery, and a lack of intentionality leads the list. Women who engage in this type of unfaithfulness don't intend to neglect their husbands; they just seem to fall into it. Maybe their mothers patterned such behavior, or perhaps their friends did. Maybe they just don't think their husbands have needs or care about relationships. Men can come across as stoic, some-times to their detriment. The wives just don't have a clue how much attention their husbands really need.

Some women neglect their husbands because their husbands have neglected them. They each get caught up in a conditional meeting of needs: I'll meet yours if you meet mine first. They miss the concept of submitting to the other's needs. They may think of their neglect as payback for all the times their husbands have neglected them, intentionally or uninten-tionally, or as a method to get their husband's attention.

Most seriously, some wives neglect their husbands out of selfishness. They get so caught up in their own lives, in their own needs, in living as they desire, that they give little atten-tion to their husbands. Their husbands rank far down the list of priorities and seem to exist only to serve the wives' needs and desires. Shannon had that attitude. She got married to meet her needs, and she fit Barry in when she had room, time, and energy.

Living the Truth

Now, let's move forward and discover how God's faithful heart can be expressed in Christian marriage.

REALIZE IT'S WRONG

Sure, everyone knows adultery is wrong, but they tend to excuse what they do as justifiable. Proverbs 30:20 (NLT) reads, "Equally amazing is how an adulterous woman can satisfy her sexual appetite, shrug her shoulders, and then say, 'What's wrong with that?'"

Many Christian women will admit their behavior is wrong, but then minimize or rationalize it. A wise person thinks about the long-term consequences of an act before engaging in it. The Bible promises some serious consequences to adultery—in any form.

First, adulterers risk their spiritual inheritance, according to 1 Corinthians 6:9-10: "Do you not know that the wicked will not inherit the kingdom of God? Do not be deceived: Neither the sexually immoral nor idolaters nor *adulterers* nor male prostitutes nor homosexual offenders nor thieves nor the greedy nor drunkards nor slanderers nor swindlers *will inherit the kingdom of God."*

That passage isn't saying that one act of unfaithfulness condemns a person forever to hell! But continued, unrepented sin indicates that an individual really doesn't desire the life of God, which will impact that person's faith relationship with him. That is a high price to pay for unfaithfulness.

Another negative consequence deals with personal integrity and reputation. Listen to this vivid scriptural description of unfaithful people: "Like a bad tooth or a lame foot is reliance on the unfaithful in times of trouble" (Proverbs 25:19).

An acquaintance of ours left his first wife for his younger secretary. She had admired him, praised him, and enticed him until he fell. After fifteen years of marriage, he hired another young secretary. Since he made good money, she likewise targeted him. Again, he fell to a younger woman. Some time later, his second wife said, "You know, I shouldn't be surprised. I did the same thing. He just can't resist young women who want him."

When marriage partners allow unfaithfulness into their lives, they become unreliable.

Another devastating result of unfaithfulness can be the destruction of the marriage. Although God certainly doesn't command that the husband of an unfaithful wife get a divorce, the option does exist. This is an option that, depending upon the depth of the damage, often occurs. Jesus said in Matthew 19:9 that divorce in this case is within the range of God's will: "I tell you that anyone who divorces his wife, *except for marital unfaithfulness*, and marries another woman commits adultery."

The momentary rush of pleasure, connection, and intimacy can cause the destruction of the marriage, damage to the children, and a serious impact on the offender's own walk with God. So the first step toward marital fidelity comes by agreeing with God that any form of adultery violates the marriage vows, breaks the heart of God, and brings damage to the lives of those affected by it.

CRAFT A STRATEGY

God encourages us not just to live reactively, not just to respond to what occurs in life, but rather to craft a strategy for life based on wisdom. We have an example of building a plan to deal with temptations toward adultery; it is found in Proverbs 2:10-11, 16: "For *wisdom* will enter your heart, and knowledge will be pleasant to your soul. Discretion will protect you, and understanding will guard you. ... It will *save you also from the adulteress*, from the wayward wife with her seductive words."

You can use God's wisdom to look at your life, recognize danger zones, and discover how you can protect yourself. Obviously, your individual strategy will differ, depending on your character, background, strengths, and weaknesses, upon your spouse, on how long the unfaithfulness has continued, and more. But we'd like to offer four steps that you can use to craft a strategy either to keep you from committing adultery, or to help you recover from it.

One quick piece of advice. Try to get a rough idea of how strongly you need to address the problem, and then double it. Even then, you'll probably need to strengthen your plan again. Why? The monster of unfaithfulness doesn't let go of us easily, and it frequently has a much stronger grip on us than we had thought.

1. Stop. Wherever you find yourself on the continuum from total faithfulness to total infidelity, whether you've just begun to fantasize or you've become actively involved, stop. When you acknowledge your sins, God is quick to forgive and restore you without condemning you. (See 1 John 1:9.) But you need to stop the behavior.

We're amazed at how Jesus balanced repentance and grace in his encounter with the woman caught in adultery. He refused to go along with the lynch-mob mentality of those who brought her to him for judgment and condemnation, but he also took her sin seriously: "'Neither do I condemn you,' Jesus declared. 'Go now and leave your life of sin'" (John 8:11). Make a conscious, deliberate decision to move away from the sin.

2. Build a new mind-set. Our attitudes and values drive our behavior. We have conversations with ourselves in our minds—*Is this wrong? How wrong? Will God forgive me? What damage might come?*—and we choose our behavior based on the outcome of those conversations. As we choose our thoughts and attitudes we shape our behavior. Jesus said in Matthew 15:19, "For *out of the heart come* evil thoughts, murder, *adultery*, sexual immorality, theft, false testimony, slander." That's why Proverbs 4:23 says, "Above all else, guard your heart, for it is the wellspring of life."

You can protect your attitudes and thoughts, your feelings and yearnings by reminding yourself regularly that you vowed faithfulness, that you long to be faithful, that devastating, if not irreparable, damage comes from giving in to temptation.

And, since God made you physical, you can use physical reminders. I (Tim) never cared much for wearing jewelry— until I got married; now I find it indispensable. If I meet a woman I'm attracted to, I rub my wedding ring to remind me of my vows. If a woman starts to flirt, I can subtly use my left hand to stroke my beard, making the ring visible, as a sign to her as well as a reminder to me.

As you choose your thoughts, you choose your behavior.

3. Identify your personal vulnerabilities. Ruthlessly look at your life and determine what settings and attitudes make you more susceptible to unfaithfulness. It may help you to remember the acronym many Twelve Step groups use, the HALT acronym. Vulnerability increases when you're Hungry, Angry, Lonely, or Tired.

Do other men look more attractive after a fight with your husband? Then resolve issues before going out into the world. Does watching certain movies or TV shows increase your romantic fantasies? Then avoid them. Think carefully about your triggers.

Then, stay alert. Don't just pick your triggers out without

putting them in an environmental context. Look for when and where they are likely to occur. Doing so allows you to minimize temptations, and we all face enough of those without looking for more. Jesus seemed aware of our struggle when he included the phrase "And lead us not into temptation, but deliver us from the evil one" in the Lord's Prayer (Matthew 6:13).

If the temptation becomes strong, run! Get out. That may mean finding a new job or a new circle of friends. Yes, you may have to make a significant sacrifice, but you must be willing to give up anything sinful in order to maintain faithfulness.

4. Build hedges of protection. Proactively build hedges ahead of time to protect yourself from temptation. Establish clear boundaries that will help you decrease the temptations in your daily life. Base these on your vulnerabilities. For example, if you know a particular television program leads you toward fantasizing about a man other than your husband, make plans that take you away from the TV at that time. If you find yourself attracted to too many activities that don't include your husband, schedule him in those activities or give them up! Also, establish a support group, some friends with whom you can talk frankly, who'll give you straight and godly advice, and to whom you'll listen. Those connections need to include confidentiality, so you'll feel safe in sharing your struggles and temptations.

EXPERIENCE RESTORATION

Any of these forms of adultery bring damage, as we've discussed. As alluring as it may seem at the moment, infidelity eventually causes damage to marriages, families, and dreams. But if you have already fallen into unfaithfulness, know that God specializes in restoring people after they have sinned. Let's look at the process.

Restoration begins with confessing that you've sinned. First, acknowledge your wrongdoing to God in order to receive his forgiveness. First John 1:9 promises, "If we confess our sins, he is faithful and just and will forgive us our sins and purify us from all unrighteousness." Trust in God's promise of forgiveness even when you don't feel like it. Don't let guilt over confessed sin bring condemnation into your life.

Next, confess the sin to those you've sinned against. That specifically includes your husband, as difficult as that may be. Jesus told us, "Therefore, if you are offering your gift at the altar and there remember that your brother [your husband] has something against you, leave your gift there in front of the altar. First go and be reconciled to your brother [your husband]; then come and offer your gift" (Matthew 5:23-24). If he won't forgive you, that becomes his problem, but make sure that you do all that you can to seek that forgiveness.

Then, forgive him for anything he may have done that increased your vulnerability. His actions don't take away your responsibility, but they can remain as a barrier if you don't address them. We can't stress enough the importance of your having a forgiving spirit. Jesus gave a hard edge to forgiveness in Matthew 6:14-15: "For if you forgive men when they sin against you, your heavenly Father will also forgive you. But if you do not forgive men their sins, your Father will not forgive your sins."

Once you've cleared the air, work on restoring the marriage relationship. Physical adultery breaks the marriage bond, and God does allow divorce for infidelity, but he longs for couples to experience restoration, a healthy marriage. In the book of Hosea, God uses the unfaithful marriage of Hosea and Gomer as a picture of the spiritual relationship between him and the nation of Israel. Gomer's repeated unfaithfulness broke the marriage bond, but read God's response: "I will betroth you to me forever; I will betroth you in righteousness and justice, in love and compassion. I will betroth you in faithfulness. ... The LORD said to me, 'Go, show your love to your wife again, though she is loved by another and is an adulteress. Love her as the LORD loves the Israelites, though they turn to other gods'" (Hosea 2:19-20; 3:1).

Exactly how you work the process of restoration depends upon the two of you and the nature and extent of the unfaithfulness. Working with a good Christian counselor can provide the insight and experience of an impartial observer. But you must begin with a desire to restore the marriage. Perhaps you can only pray, "God, I don't want to go through the pain of working this out. But I'm willing to let you change my heart." If so, begin with that willingness to be made willing.

David is a wonderful example of true repentance. He committed adultery and even had the woman's husband killed to cover it up. For about a year he saw nothing wrong with what he'd done. Read 2 Samuel 11 and 12 and Psalm 51 to see David's realization that he had seriously sinned, his humble repentance before God, and the spiritual restoration he experienced. After this experience, as tragic as it was and as painful as its consequences were, David went on to have a good marriage, served as the spiritual leader of Israel, and wrote a number of psalms.

Yes, adultery in any form is wrong. Yes, as a Christian wife you must avoid it. But if you have already fallen into adultery, you can experience God's forgiveness and restoration. And that's the truth.

Lie 6

Nothing's Wrong; I'm Just Fine

The Truth about Direct Communication

"H"ey man, you're late. Anything wrong?" Sweat dripped off Alex after fifteen minutes on the treadmill. "Dude, you wouldn't believe it. But then, you're married, so maybe you will." Don stepped onto the adjoining treadmill and started running.

"I got home from work today and grabbed my gym clothes like I do every Tuesday. Shontell seemed distant, like she'd had another bad day at work. Her boss has been putting a lot of pressure on her to finish that condominium project, and I'm kinda concerned. The baby's due date is still four months away, but I just don't want her to feel any unnecessary stress.

"So I go up to her, give her a hug, and ask if anything's wrong. 'No, I'm fine, just fine.' You know how women say *fine*, with that short, cut-off stress on the *i*? So I told her she could talk to me; I'm her husband. Know what I heard? 'Go. Just go. You're late for your workout with Alex.'

"So I went! But I know I'm going to hear it when I get back. I don't have a clue if it's something wrong at work, or if I did something, but I know it's not over yet."

"Man, why can't women just come out and say what they mean? Danielle does the same thing. We had our tenth anniversary a few weeks back, remember? So a few weeks ahead, I asked her what she'd like to make it special. I'd saved up some extra money just to do it right. She said, 'Just surprise me! The greatest gift is our marriage.'

"I remember I'd heard her talking to a friend about this bed and breakfast inn down the coast. A little pricey, but nice. So I made the reservations, let her know the kind of clothes to bring, and surprised her. She said all the right things, how nice it was, how I surprised her, but her heart didn't seem to be in it.

"I asked her what was wrong, and she kept saying, 'Nothing.' Finally, the last day there, she told me she really had her heart set on a new wedding ring. How was I supposed to know that? She's *never* said anything about a new ring. Man, I can't figure out women. They just don't say what they mean. They hint, and they want you to read their mind. Then you try to, and you get crucified. Why can't they just tell us straight?"

The Lie

Wives typically use indirect forms of communication. They give hints, they speak abstractly, and then they expect their husbands to know what they mean. Without ever intending to lie, they don't express the full truth. At times, they communicate so indirectly that their husbands can't come close to perceiving the real message.

When they say, "Nothing's wrong; I'm just fine," they may mean that message as indirect communication, but the fact is that it is a lie.

Behind the Lie

Women communicate indirectly for a variety of factors, and any combination may come into play. We encourage both husbands and wives to carefully think about why the truth doesn't get stated directly and clearly. As they discover the why, they can understand the other person better and over-come the hurdles to direct communication.

DIFFERENT COMMUNICATION STYLES

Women tend to have more skill in verbal communication; they pick up the various layers of meaning in a communication event much more effectively than men. That's why women can accurately finish the sentences of their female friends; they understand indirect communication better than their male counterparts.

Indirect messages don't explicitly give meaning, they imply it, and they have several advantages. Speaking indirectly a woman can ask for a compliment without appearing to do so. "Do you like this dress I just bought?" can prompt the desired response of "Oh yes, you look stunning in it!"

Indirect messages can increase politeness. Instead of saying, "I can't stand your mother and will not spend an entire weekend with her," a wife can say, "I'd love to stay at your mom's for the weekend, but I already committed to work in the nursery on Sunday morning, and none of the other workers is available."

However, indirect messages can be thought of as manipulative, since the speaker tries to get the hearer to do something without directly asking. The next chapter covers this subject in depth. Additionally, the person who uses indirect messages runs the risk of not providing clear communication. The receiver may simply fail to pick up what the sender wants to convey.

Wives may use indirect communication because they understand it well, not realizing it can be a foreign language to husbands.

UNCERTAINTY

Sometimes women speak indirectly because they don't quite have all their thoughts sorted out yet. They may say, "Nothing's wrong; I'm just fine," but they mean, "Yes, something's wrong; I'm not fine, but I can't begin to put it into words yet." Are their words inaccurate? Of course. The meaning of the words contradicts the thoughts behind them.

Hormonal changes can put women on an emotional

roller coaster that they can't always figure out or articulate. Husbands have a difficult time understanding what women feel at these times. Husbands know it's real—they experience the results—but they just can't personally experience the hormonal changes that impact women.

One husband gamely tried to get beyond what his wife thought and asked, "What emotions do you feel now?"

She snapped back, "I don't know what I'm feeling. You tell me."

Sometimes the indirect statement "Nothing's wrong" means "Nothing's wrong that I feel ready to talk about yet."

AN UNSAFE ENVIRONMENT

Some women hide the truth out of fear that speaking it won't be safe. The husband may get defensive and argue against it. I (Tim) did that a lot in our earlier years. More than once Sheila accused me of looking at another woman inappropriately, and I disagreed and gave all the reasons I hadn't done so. I had a hard time acknowledging weaknesses and failures, so I just wouldn't admit to them. Many husbands share that flaw, and after a while, some wives don't tell why they're upset because they know it won't do any good. They just give up the fight.

Other husbands take it even further—into abuse. They live in denial and don't want to acknowledge problems, and they can become verbally or physically abusive when confronted with them. We want to make it abundantly clear: you do not have to put up with abuse. We encourage you to find professional help such as counseling for verbal abuse, and to get to a safe environment if you are a victim of physical abuse.

CONFLICT AVOIDANCE

Several communication studies indicate that women approach conflict more openly, while men tend to withdraw. Women often view conflict as a means of resolving relationship stress; men often see it as increasing stress. However, a study on the "Spiral of Silence" theory published by Elisabeth

Noelle-Neumann in 1991[1] indicates that women are less likely than men to express a minority opinion. Or, if they anticipate the husband (and others) as potentially disagreeing with them, they may withdraw from the conflict.

We can perhaps explain that reaction by reference to a study conducted by Rachel Rosenfeld in 1979, which revealed that women may avoid self-disclosure if it has the potential to damage a relationship.[2] Wives may use indirect language at times to avoid bringing out in the open conflicts that can hurt the marriage.

For seven years, Tim pastored a church in Rancho Palos Verdes while we lived in Temecula, about a hundred miles away. We'd spend most of Sunday at the church and then would begin the hour-and-a-half trip home. One nice afternoon Tim suggested that we drive down the Southern California coast, a gorgeous drive but one that added an hour to our trip. My fibromyalgia was acting up, so I said, "Let's just go home, okay?"

A few weeks later Tim suggested the coast route again, and although I definitely wanted to get home as soon as possible, I said, "If you really want to." I hoped Tim would recognize my hesitancy and take the quicker route home. But I didn't want to make an issue out of it because I feared it would just add more tension to our marriage, which had enough already at that point.

On the Receiving End

When faced with indirect communication, husbands often feel like a one-legged man in a football kicking contest. They just don't have what it takes. They much prefer dealing with facts, logic, and problem solving.

They notice that something is wrong. That realization may come from receiving the silent treatment, getting some indirect messages, or just picking up the mood of their wife. They'd like to resolve the problem, so they ask about it, and get messages so indirect that they can't interpret their meaning. One husband, Trace, said, "If I did something wrong, I want to fix it. But if she won't clearly tell me what I did, I can never do better. I get so frustrated."

Ray, another husband, told of how his wife seemed uneasy but used the classic line, "I'm just fine." A few days later she told him about some friction she'd had with a friend, but she hadn't come close to processing it fully and hadn't wanted to talk about it when he asked. "Why couldn't she have just said, 'I'm stressed over something Kathy did, but I don't want to talk about it now'? I felt bad for three days! I thought I'd done something wrong and was trying to figure what it was. I'd have been a whole lot better off if she'd just said what she meant."

When people get what they see as an incomplete message, they try to fill in the blanks. Husbands, with their strong problem-resolution skills, will often explore various possible meanings. But if the indirect message doesn't have enough clues to give them an accurate picture, they can't succeed.

Living the Truth

Neither indirect nor direct communication is intrinsically right or wrong. Rather, each serves a particular purpose. Foundationally, though, wives make a mistake when they choose indirect messages that give a misleading impression, or that fail to accurately convey the intended meaning. Let's explore six factors that can help you live in the truth and communicate more directly.

UNDERSTAND GOD'S COMMUNICATION PATTERN

As Christians, we want to follow the example of God, who highly values communication. He created the world by speaking. He communicated what he expected from his people by prophets. The Bible even calls his only Son "the Word." So, let's survey how he communicates.

On key truths, God consistently communicates directly. In the Garden of Eden, he clearly told Adam and Eve what he expected from them: "But the LORD God gave him [Adam] this warning: 'You [and your wife] may freely eat any fruit in the garden except fruit from the tree of the knowledge of good and evil. If you eat of its fruit, you will surely die'" (Genesis 2:16-17 NLT). Nothing could be more direct and clear than that! God clearly defined wrong by just one act that he described explicitly. Later, when he established the descendants of Abraham in the Promised Land, God again made his message clear:

> "'You yourselves have seen what I did to Egypt, and how I carried you on eagles' wings and brought you to myself. Now if you obey me fully and keep my covenant, then out of all nations you will be my treasured possession. Although the whole earth is mine, you will be for me a kingdom of priests and a holy nation.'" (Exodus 19:4-6)

He followed that instruction with the Ten Commandments, the principal foundation of the covenant relationship. He then amplified the Big Ten with a total of 631 specific commandments, just in the first five books of the Old Testament. Again, it's impossible to get much more direct and clear than that!

When the people of God strayed, he sent prophets to remind them of their obligation to him. One example is Hosea. The people had substituted a legalistic following of rules for a relationship of knowing God. Through his prophet he said to them, "I want you to be merciful; I don't want your sacrifices. I want you to know God; that's more important than burnt offerings. But like Adam, you broke my covenant and rebelled against me" (Hosea 6:6-7 NLT).

God communicated with a clear statement of what he desired. Then, when the people either didn't understand it or willfully violated it, he restated it. He communicated directly and clearly so his people would know just what he wanted and expected. Should his children do any less in their marriages? We encourage couples to commit to direct and clear communication between themselves to avoid the possibility of misunderstanding. God has set the example for his children to follow.

CREATE A SAFE ZONE

Husband, creating a communication "safe zone" is your job. Yes, you get frustrated and upset at indirect conversation. But some of your irritation results from your own response when your wife tries to communicate with you. When you create a safe zone, your wife can more easily speak directly. Once I (Tim) quit being defensive and arguing against what she saw, Sheila found it much easier to bring up issues. My non-defensive response lowered the emotional level of the confrontation, and we could deal with the issue at hand more rationally and directly.

You can create a safe zone in several ways. First, choose honesty over defending yourself. Nothing works like honesty to disarm a volatile situation with a spouse. Don't make excuses, don't rationalize. Just own up to your role, to what you did. Don't accept blame for what you didn't do, however, since that won't help to resolve the real issue. When you build a reputation for owning up to your mistakes, your wife will more likely believe you when you refuse to accept responsibility for something you didn't do.

Second, don't respond with an attack on your wife. Citing her bad behavior doesn't negate your bad behavior. Yes, it can work to divert her attention from the issue at hand because the best defense is a good offense, but you'll merely encourage her to continue to speak indirectly, and you will both lose in the long term.

Third, don't even think about verbal or physical abuse. Men often have a vocal strength that intimidates women, and a lot of men use that advantage intentionally. It scares their wives into indirect messages, and as a result few issues get resolved. Of course, physical abuse should have no place at all in a marriage. If you've resorted to violence to solve problems, or almost have, get professional help. Now.

Fourth, draw out your wife with active listening. Rephrase what she said: "Honey, did you say that you resent my mom because of how controlling she is?" Ask questions that probe below the surface to encourage more direct communication: "Can you give a specific time when Mom acted in a controlling manner?"

Let your wife know that you truly want to hear what she has to say, and when she sees that you've established a safe zone, you should see an increase in the clarity of your communication with one another.

RECOGNIZE DANGER ZONES

Communication becomes dangerous when it's unclear or misleading. Recognizing that fact can motivate you and your spouse to speak more clearly and beneficially. Let's examine how and why communication can become a danger and what can be done to minimize that danger.

First, dangerous messages give the wrong impression. Our words might be technically accurate, but they may be intended to deceive. Or, we can purposely misstate the truth. First Peter 3:10 cautions us: "Whoever would love life and see good days must keep his tongue from evil and his lips from *deceitful speech*."

Peter associated misleading speech with evil, and contrasted it with a passion for life and enjoyment. Why? Perhaps because when we deceive, we eliminate the chances of resolving an issue since we won't state it directly. The problem and its pain continue to plague us. They deny reality.

Second, dangerous messages take reckless risks with a marriage. They put trust at risk; they put intimacy at risk: "Reckless words pierce like a sword, but the tongue of the wise brings healing" (Proverbs 12:18). Wise words can heal problems in a marriage, but indirect messages can cut the heart of a spouse and jeopardize the relationship.

Third, dangerous messages may increase miscommunication between marriage partners. Often this occurs when spouses don't take time to evaluate their thoughts and feelings, their partner, and their marriage. "My dear brothers, take note of this: Everyone should be quick to listen, *slow to speak* and slow to become angry" (James 1:19). Husbands must fully understand that wives may not be ready to talk over an issue, and at that point restraint may be the height of wisdom! But wives must realize that indirect language that indicates nothing is wrong doesn't represent the truth!

SHARE THE POWER OF A COMMON LANGUAGE

Words have power—for good or for bad. As we've mentioned, the words of God brought the universe into existence. Four simple words—*Will you marry me?*—followed by one more word—*yes*—can change a multitude of lives. When we use words well, their power transforms us for good. When we use words poorly, their power transforms us for evil.

In the first book of the Bible we see an intriguing example of the power of words. When God grew concerned about the ability of people to build a tower reaching the heavens he identified one source of their success in wrongdoing: "The LORD said, 'If as *one people speaking the same language* they have begun to do this, then nothing they plan to do will be impossible for them. Come, let us go down and confuse their language so *they will not understand each other*'" (Genesis 11:6-7).

Notice that a common language brought unity; it allowed a group of individuals to become one people. That unity provided power—in this case, the power to do evil. So what did God do? To weaken them, he kept them from understanding each other. Doesn't that represent the situation in many marriages today? When one speaks indirectly and the other doesn't understand the meaning, then the couple's unity becomes diminished, and the power to achieve their best decreases.

We encourage couples to use a common language, one the other can clearly recognize and understand. Wife, this primarily depends on you. Being female, you probably have more communication skills than your husband, so follow the principle set forth by the apostle Paul in Romans 15:1-2: "We who are strong ought to bear with the failings of the weak and not to please ourselves. Each of us should please his neighbor for his good, to build him up."

Make an extra effort to speak so your husband can understand you. You can speak his direct language much easier than he can understand your indirect language. Speaking a common language will allow you both to follow the next principle.

SPEAK THE FULL TRUTH—IN LOVE

Probably the greatest concern about indirect messages deals with their potential to convey either less than the full truth or complete untruth. They have a great ability to mislead and to create misunderstanding. Think back to Danielle's statement to Alex that led to their anniversary being less special than it could have been.

When you create a safe zone, recognize the dangers of indirect communication, and commit to speaking a common language, then you can risk speaking the full truth. That's biblical. As we have seen, in Ephesians 4:15, 25 the apostle Paul encouraged us: "Instead, *speaking the truth in love*, we will in all things grow up into him who is the Head, that is, Christ. ... Therefore each of you must put off falsehood and *speak truthfully* to his neighbor, for we are all *members of one body*."

Husbands and wives are members of one body in more ways than members of the church, which gives them even more motivation to speak the truth. Remember, misleading or lying diminishes unity.

You don't have to tell everybody everything to be truthful! If you're still in the process of working through your thoughts and emotions, don't say, "Nothing's wrong; I'm just fine." You're not fine, so be honest with yourself and your spouse. Say that you are dealing with a situation you can't talk about right now, but that you will do so as soon as you have sorted it out. That's truth.

Now, let's summarize the main points of this chapter.

SPEAK CLEARLY AND DIRECTLY

God communicates clearly and directly, and he wants his children to do the same. At times Jesus did speak indirectly, but with his closest followers he spoke very clearly. In John 16, his disciples didn't quite follow some of what he had said, so they asked him to clarify his meaning. In verse 25 he responded to their question: "Though I have been speaking figuratively, a time is coming when I will no longer use this kind of language but will *tell you plainly* about my Father."

Jesus went on to speak very directly about the Father, and the disciples got it in verse 29: "Now you are *speaking clearly* and without figures of speech."

At another time, Jesus encouraged his followers to be truthful, trustworthy, and clear:

> Again, you have heard that it was said to the people long ago, "Do not break your oath, but keep the oaths you have made to the Lord." But I tell you, Do not swear at all: either by heaven, for it is God's throne; or by the earth, for it is his footstool; or by Jerusalem, for it is the city of the Great King. And do not swear by your head, for you cannot make even one hair white or black. Simply let your "Yes" be "Yes," and your "No," "No"; anything beyond this comes from the evil one. (Matthew 5:33–37)

Wife, your husband needs your help. Try to speak directly. Phrase your requests in terms he can understand. Do your best to avoid figurative language. Following these directives won't guarantee that you'll get what you want, but it should increase the chances.

Speaking a common language can increase your unity and your strength as a couple. And that's the truth.

Lie 7

I Don't Need Your Help; I Can Take Care of It

The Truth about Communicating Needs

Jillian and Marc followed their typical Saturday morning routine: they got up when their bodies said "enough" to sleep, started the coffeemaker, and toasted a couple of bagels. They leisurely read the paper and enjoyed the morning sun streaming through the windows of the breakfast nook.

Jillian put down her paper to look at the birds outside and said, "Hey, look at those dirty windows."

Marc glanced up from the sports page—his beloved Lakers had lost again—saw what looked like a few water spots, and replied, "Yeah, I guess the sprinkler system hit them a little. Must have been a breeze," and he returned to his paper.

Jillian silently stewed. Marc always ignored her requests to do something around the house. She wanted him to clean the windows. She wanted him to fix the sprinkler system, and he just shined her on. Again. Did he just not care about her? About the work that he needed to do?

Several years ago, our daughter got married on May 16, and my (Sheila's) family came out to the West Coast several weeks early. I told Tim that with the wedding expenses and the busyness of the moment, not to get me anything nor to do anything for my fiftieth birthday only five days later. Just a card would be fine.

Like a typical husband, he did exactly what I said. No more. I discovered that I resented him for it because deep down I really wanted him to do something special. After all, fiftieth birthdays don't come very often! If he really knew me, I reasoned, he should have known that the day was important to me.

Now, he did throw a big surprise birthday bash when I turned sixty, and that helped. But I still remember the disappointment I felt when he ignored my fiftieth birthday—just as I had asked him to do.

The Lie

Wives speak less than the truth when they don't clearly spell out their requests, when they assume that their husbands know what they really want. Our last lie explored the need for direct communication in general; this one delves into making specific requests. And generally insincere statements like, "I don't really need your help; I can take care of it" used instead of direct requests are not just incomplete truths, they are actually lies.

Behind the Lie

When Jillian mentioned the dirty windows, she really wanted Marc both to wash the windows and to fix the sprinklers. When Sheila told Tim to do nothing for her birthday, she really wanted him to see behind her sacrificial statement and show how special she was to him.

Studies consistently reveal that men and women communicate differently. Three primary factors lead wives to express their needs in an indirect manner.

GENDER DIFFERENCES

Joseph DeVito, in his book *Human Communication*, cites a 1995 study by J. Holmes that suggests three causes of communication differences in men and women.[1] First, *innate biological differences* contribute; differences in politeness and listening may come from biology.

Socialization also contributes, because boys and girls are taught to communicate in different ways. *Social power* plays a role. Those with lesser social power, typically females, often communicate with greater deference and politeness. This factor particularly encourages wives to present indirect requests rather than direct ones.

These three causes—biological differences, socialization, and social power—combine to yield two very distinct communication styles, styles that affect how women communicate to men in two primary ways.

SELF-DISCLOSURE HESITANCY

Although studies affirm that women tend to disclose information about themselves more than men do, women often avoid disclosing such personal information in certain instances. DeVito cites a 1979 study by Rosenfeld that suggests this avoidance occurs when women feel the information may be used against them or if it may hurt their relationships with others.[2]

When the wife asks clearly for something, she places the husband in a position of power: he can choose to grant or deny the request. If she couches her request in an observation, she lowers her risk of negative consequences.

UNSTATED EXPECTATIONS

I (Tim) remember trying to follow conversations between my mother and her lifelong friend and next-door neighbor. Mom and Phyllis would finish each other's sentences, hearing only a few phrases and still getting the meaning. I couldn't even figure out the subject, let alone the specifics. Women do really well at that type of conversation; men don't. Wives do better at reading the context and discerning and deciphering emotional messages in a conversation.

Because women have better communication skills than men do, they often expect their husbands to "read their minds," much like their female friends do, much like Sheila expected Tim to do something for her birthday even though she had told him not to. Women somehow think that several years of marriage should give their husbands some secret knowledge about their often unspoken desires and dreams.

But guys are just guys. They don't have any secret knowledge. In fact, they don't even know there is any secret knowledge! If men are asked to fix something, most of them will at least give it a shot. But if they are expected to instinctively know what their wives are thinking, they are doomed to failure.

On the Receiving End

Men tend to communicate on a fact basis, and they respond to statements of fact on a factual level. So when Jillian said the windows were dirty, Marc gave an entirely appropriate response—on a factual level. He agreed that there were some water spots on the windows, and he even diagnosed the cause of the problem: the sprinkler system. Conversation successfully concluded. And when Sheila said she didn't want him to do anything for her birthday, Tim viewed that statement as an entirely logical request that he could fulfill. Conversation successfully concluded.

Later, when the wives say what they really desired, husbands tend to get confused. "But why didn't you just say that? I would have been glad to do it if you'd just asked."

The encounter often escalates as the women, who perceived that their husbands ignored their requests, express their frustrations. Some, like Jillian, generalize the one situation into major relationship issues.

One of the men said, "I feel like I can't win. If I take her statement at face value, she gets mad because I don't do anything. But she never asks me to do anything. And if I can't figure out what she really wants, then I'm an insensitive clod who doesn't know her."

So far, we have a recipe for frustration. The wives express their needs in an indirect manner they think should be understood. The husbands typically don't receive the intended message. The wives get frustrated, and the husbands get confused. Both need to learn to communicate more clearly.

Living the Truth

We'd like to suggest four steps that can help couples communicate more clearly. Particularly, following these steps can help wives not only express themselves more effectively to their husbands, but also give them the best chance possible of having their requests granted and their needs met.

The verses we use primarily refer to our relationship with God, but we'd like to assume that the basic principles apply to the marriage relationship as well. After all, doesn't God frequently compare his relationship with us to marriage? We won't take it too far, but we do think that God's love for us sets the pattern for how we are to love one another.

MAKE YOUR REQUESTS KNOWN

In John 16:24, Jesus encouraged us to ask so that our needs may be met. "Ask and you will receive, and your joy will be complete." Again, this verse refers primarily to asking our heavenly Father, not our earthly husband. Asking doesn't guarantee getting, but not asking pretty much does guarantee not getting.

Jabez provides a classic example of asking. "Jabez cried out to the God of Israel, 'Oh, that you would bless me and enlarge my territory! Let your hand be with me, and keep me from harm so that I will be free from pain.' And God granted his request" (1 Chronicles 4:10). That's about all we are told about Jabez. But what a reputation he has! He made a request of God, and God granted it.

Wife, make requests to your husband. But when you do, realize that he is a man, and you need to communicate with him in a manner that a man can understand. That leads to the next steps.

BE DIRECT AND CLEAR

Jesus encouraged clear and direct communication in Matthew 5:37: "Simply let your 'Yes' be 'Yes,' and your 'No,' 'No.'" Don't equivocate, don't sugarcoat, don't be subtle. Rather, put your requests in simple, direct, and clear terms.

Let's go back to our opening scenario. Jillian would have been much more likely to have her request met if she had phrased her part of the conversation differently. Let's try a second take with Marc and Jillian.

"Hey, look at those dirty windows."

"Yeah, I guess the sprinkler system hit them a little. Must have been a breeze."

"Marc, when you finish the paper, could you please wash the windows and get the sprinkler system aligned?"

"Sure, it shouldn't take too long. I can do that before I mow the lawn."

"Thanks. I know you've had a long week. I appreciate your taking the time to do the things that are important to me."

Now, does Jillian's phrasing guarantee that Marc will respond in the way she wants him to? Of course not. But it does improve her odds.

I (Tim) would have responded differently back on Sheila's fiftieth birthday if she had said something like this: "Tim, we've been really busy with Teri's wedding and with my mom and sis out here. And I know it hit our finances too. Instead of a gift for my birthday, why don't the two of us drive down the coast, have a nice dinner somewhere, and watch the sunset? I think I'd like that kind of a birthday this year."

With communication like that, I wouldn't have basically ignored her birthday, she wouldn't have been disappointed, and I would have known pretty clearly what she really wanted.

Wife, don't give subtle hints. Husbands don't do subtle very well. Dr. Laura Schlessinger quoted a woman named Mary on this subject: "It's amazing how I let myself get irritated if a laundry basket … stayed at the foot of the stairs. … I expected him to know that I thought he should put [it] away. Now I just tell him the laundry … is clean and ask him if he would please take it with him … the next time he goes upstairs. And he does it with no problem!"[3]

A laundry basket at the foot of the stairs doesn't register on a husband's radar. Mary's husband didn't intend to upset her; he gladly took care of the clothes once she asked him. But she had to make her request clear and direct.

Also, try to make just one or two requests at a time. Husbands don't multitask as well as women, and they're apt to forget.

BE LOVING, NOT CRITICAL

Men respond well to appreciation and admiration. They resist negativity and a critical spirit. In our revised opening scenario, Jillian incorporated a loving spirit. She made a request, not a demand. She also added some appreciation, acknowledging Marc's busy schedule and thanking him for making her needs a priority.

GIVE GENTLE REMINDERS

Let's face it. Men don't always do what they say they will. They start one task, get distracted by another, and the first goes out the window. Or, they agree to the request and kind of mean to do it, but it doesn't fully register on their agenda. Or, they just plain forget.

They're imperfect. Even when wives communicate their desires and needs clearly and directly, their husbands still may not get the message; and even if they do get the message, they still may not always do what was asked of them. So rather than letting your aggravation grow, give some gentle reminders. You don't need to take it to the level of a nagging offense, but you don't want to let your husband forget it entirely either. So a gentle reminder or two shouldn't be a problem.

We've written this book on the premise that both husbands and wives want a good marriage, that both basically want to meet the needs of the other. When wives express their requests in clear, direct, and loving terms, those requests get met—not always, of course, but much more often. And that's the truth.

Lie 8

We Just Don't Have Anything in Common Anymore

The Truth about Personal Intimacy

Sean fussed and cried almost all night long. He wasn't hungry, wet, or hurting; he just wanted to be picked up. Sarah had gotten almost no sleep, so she knew she'd be fighting fatigue and dragging around the house all day. She got the two older kids off to school, fed the baby, and put him down for a nap. Next came several loads of laundry. She lay down for fifteen minutes after lunch and then started dinner.

She picked up Chelsea from play practice and Lindsey from a soccer game, and had just gotten the table set when Lloyd walked in from work—with that little glimmer in his eye. Her heart sank. Didn't he think of anything else? Didn't he have a clue what she felt? They got through dinner, got the kids to bed, did the dishes together, and then he put his arms around her. "Feel like going to bed early ourselves?"

The chronic fatigue that weighed her down, what she perceived as her husband's lack of sensitivity to her needs, and ten years of marriage, housework, and child rearing combined to cause the eruption.

"You don't have a clue, do you?" she exploded. "You're caught up with your job; I'm caught up with the kids. I spend my day taking care of them, cooking, keeping the house, and running errands. You come home from work, we eat, you work on a project out in the garage, and then you expect me to just jump up and run to the bedroom with you.

"I loved the way we spent time together when we started dating. We'd talk for hours, and you'd listen. You really did. You asked questions about what I thought, what I liked, what my dreams were. I can't remember the last time you did that. We used to take day trips together; we're lucky to get a night out now.

"Face it, Lloyd. We've grown apart. We share a house and the kids, and you want us to share sex. You'll help with the dishes, but that's about it. Our marriage has become a sham. We just don't have anything in common anymore."

The Lie

Sarah's frustration was entirely real. But was her statement true? Did she and Lloyd really have nothing in common? True, because they had far fewer activities in common than they had previously. True, because they had far less in common than she desired. False, because they did share more than the house, kids, and occasional sex. False, because she expected more intimacy in marriage than any husband could provide.

Basically, Sarah's misconception came from expecting her marriage to meet all her needs for intimacy.

Behind the Lie

Husbands typically have no idea how deep the need for intimacy runs in their wives. Husbands are often baffled by it, since their focus tends to be more on activity, on doing, while their wives tend to focus more on building relationships, on being. Not only are husbands surprised by the intensity of their wives' need, they are also shocked that their wives expect them to meet it! Three major factors contribute to the expectation of wives for so much intimacy from their husbands.

A HEART FOR INTIMACY

All people need intimate relationships, with intimacy expressed in a variety of ways. Webster's dictionary gives the root of the word *intimate* as "innermost."[1] It could be said that intimate relationships touch the very core of a person. WordNet uses a quote that associates intimacy with "an absence of fences."[2] Intimacy thus allows couples to reach inside one another and access what would normally be closely guarded.

Wives yearn for four dimensions of intimacy in their marriages.

Emotional intimacy involves a feeling of connectedness and romance, of feeling cherished and special.

Spiritual intimacy relates to the nonmaterial aspects of the couple's relationship, especially in regard to God. It doesn't just mean that the husband and wife each know God, but that they connect with one another in their spiritual lives. That doesn't necessarily require that they pray together every day, but they should talk about their spiritual journeys, the joys and difficulties, and share a common heart for the things of God.

Mental intimacy refers to conversation, to shared thoughts and reflections, to open minds toward each other. That WordNet reference to the absence of fences fits here. Couples with mental intimacy can talk about a variety of subjects without causing pain, embarrassment, resentment, or conflict.

Physical intimacy (here we go, guys!) obviously involves sex, but it really focuses on the greater issue of physical presence and touching. For many wives, just being together goes a long way toward meeting some of their intimacy needs. Wives appreciate nonsexual touches that don't communicate a desire for sex but for closeness. Holding hands, hugging, wrapping an arm around the shoulders all fit in this category.

LOOKING IN THE WRONG PLACES

A song written by Waylan Jennings that was popular several years ago was titled "Looking for Love in All the Wrong Places." Wives may do the same with intimacy when they expect their husbands to meet the preponderance of their intimacy needs. Dr. James Dobson talked about this subject in his first video series, "Focus on the Family."[3] Just a few generations ago, extended families lived close together, and the neighbor-hood wives got together for coffee. Those "girl times" went a long way toward meeting all four types of intimacy needs. The women could connect emotionally as friends, spiritually when they talked on the same spiritual wavelength, mentally through conversation, and even physically with the hugs and kisses that women so often give one another.

With the fragmenting of families, however, with couples moving around the country, and with so many wives working full-time jobs outside the home, many of those opportunities have decreased or even vanished altogether. Wives now expect their husbands to meet those needs and often believe that their marriages are poor when their husbands fail to meet this unre-alistic expectation.

LIVING SEPARATE LIVES

Many wives accurately diagnose their marital problems as a lack of intimacy. When dating, couples are consumed with one another. Tim and Sheila remember staying up until two or three in the morning—on work nights—just talking and getting to know one another. But once the couple marries, the emotional rush fades, and the two partners begin to drift apart. Children often suck up huge amounts of time that used to be devoted to the marriage. Careers demand more time and energy. Outside activities, whether related to church, recre-ation, or friends, pull couples apart.

Although Sarah claimed that she and Lloyd had nothing in common anymore, she was only partly wrong. In one way she hit the nail on the head. They didn't share as much time and activities with just the two of them as they had done before. They still shared many things, but not as many as previously.

RESULTS

Needs are needs, and when they are not met, wives either operate on a deficit or look elsewhere for fulfillment. Operating on a deficit can cause wives to withdraw from their marriage relationships; they give up on getting their needs met at home. Also it increases their vulnerability. When they begin to look to others outside the marriage to meet their needs for intimacy, temptation greatly increases.

On the Receiving End

Husbands typically feel bewildered when confronted by statements from their wives that they share nothing in common anymore. One husband, Jim, said, "What does she want? I work hard to provide a home for my family. I'm there. I do my part. For heaven's sake, we're not teenagers anymore. We haven't just fallen in love. We've got some miles on our relationship. Just because I'm not all lovey-dovey doesn't mean I don't love her. Our love has just matured, that's all."

Part of the problem comes from men defining intimacy differently than women. Jared, another husband, expressed his view of togetherness: "I love it when we sit together and watch sports. That's pretty much all it takes to make me content. My wife and I sitting together on the couch, a football game on TV. Just being together. But she's up and down, starting this job, finishing another. Why can't she just sit down with me?"

When wives feel that their husbands don't meet their needs for intimacy, they become more vulnerable. But when the wives withdraw from the relationship, it also leaves their husbands more vulnerable. Their companionship needs aren't being met, and they become more susceptible to those outside the marriage who can provide what they seek in that area.

Living the Truth

Now, let's explore three steps that couples can take to better understand and achieve intimacy.

UNDERSTAND YOUR NEED FOR IT

A need for connecting on an intimate level lies at the heart of every human. We may put up fences to protect our innermost person, but we all yearn for someone who loves us enough, and is safe enough, to allow us to take down those fences. We've frequently used Genesis 2:18 (NLT), which discusses how God recognized the human need for connecting with another human: "It is not good for the man to be alone. I will make *a companion who will help him."*

In the Garden, Adam enjoyed tremendous spiritual, emotional, and mental intimacy while in the physical presence of God. But that didn't meet all of his needs for intimacy. He needed a companion like himself, so God said, "I will make him a helper *comparable* to him" (NKJV).

We've said that wives fall prey to a misconception that their husbands can meet all of their intimacy needs. But the husbands need to meet only the primary intimacy needs of their wives, and those needs flow from God's original creation design. Recognizing the human need for intimacy with another human, God took the next step. From Adam's rib God crafted another form of human—a woman—and then gave the blueprint for how they would connect and meet one another's intimacy needs. "For this reason a man will leave his father and mother and be united to his wife, and they will become one flesh. The man and his wife were both naked, and they felt no shame" (Genesis 2:24–25).

Notice the marvelous pattern! First, the husband and wife leave other primary relationships and make their marriage their main source of intimacy. Not sole, as we'll explore later, but primary. Their commitment leads to the next stage of intimacy: they unite so deeply that they become one. The Bible also uses that word *one* to describe how the Father, Son, and Spirit are one, such as in Deuteronomy 6:4: "Hear, O Israel: The LORD our God, the LORD is one."

This deep union allows nakedness and removes the fences—physical, emotional, mental, and spiritual—that keep their spouse from seeing them as they really are.

Do all marriages reach this level of intimacy? No, because the effects of the Fall in the Garden of Eden continue to impact marriages. It's not surprising that the primary relationship God designed for people would become a spiritual battleground that can bring more frustration and pain than just about anything else. The potential of the pain, however, matches the potential of the gain.

What did God give as the reason for this intimacy? That marriage would become the primary place for people to take down their fences, to have a life companion who would see into the deepest parts of their soul and still love them.

And although many men resist this kind of intimacy, they need it just as much as their wives do. They just need it in different ways. Many women spell intimacy c-o-n-v-e-r-s-a-t-i-o-n. Many men spell it c-o-m-p-a-n-i-o-n-s-h-i-p or s-e-x. But the underlying need remains the same: connecting with another human being in the innermost areas of the soul.

So the first step toward shared intimacy is to realize that we all need intimacy—husbands and wives alike. But you must also realize that the marriage cannot be your only source for intimacy.

DEVELOP A VARIETY OF INTIMATE RELATIONSHIPS

Husbands operate on such a different wavelength that they often cannot fully understand and empathize with their wives. This male mind-set requires wives to develop a support system of intimate relationships that will supplement the marriage. We suggest developing intimacy in four dimensions. Each of these four will provide its unique contribution to the fulfillment of intimacy needs. None of them can do it all, but all can do some.

First, *get to know God intimately*. God won't directly meet all your relationship needs, but he can touch you in ways that no human can. God has always desired intimacy with his people. Jews prayed this prayer on a daily basis: "Hear, O Israel: The LORD our God, the LORD is one. Love the LORD your God with all your heart and with all your soul and with all your strength" (Deuteronomy 6:4–5). Now that's intimacy!

Books abound that will guide you into developing more intimacy with God, which is vital, because unless you build a solid connection with God, your need for spiritual intimacy cannot be met. Knowing God closely provides the security you need to explore intimacy in other areas.

Second, *get to know your spouse intimately*. Our next section will give some practical tips on how to develop this intimacy. As we've said before, your marriage should provide the bulk of intimacy in your shared life, which matches God's design from the Garden days. As spouses, you should strive to develop all four dimensions of intimacy: physical, emotional, mental, and spiritual.

The social penetration theory of communication suggests that the depth of any relationship depends upon the degree to which each partner penetrates to the core of the other.[4] Restated, the more a couple shares their innermost persons (they more they develop shared intimacy), the deeper their marriage relationship will be.

Third, *develop some intimate friendships*. Friends of the same gender can provide some excellent peer-to-peer connections for each of the marriage partners. Such friends understand the partner's thought processes, they know the partner's history, and the partner can feel safe with them. Proverbs 18:24 talks about the difference between companions and friends: "A man of many companions may come to ruin, but there is a friend who sticks closer than a brother."

Friends get beneath the surface, they love unconditionally, and they can ask the hard questions. I (Sheila) have a number of close friendships, and I've discovered that each friend plays a unique and different role in my life. No one friend can meet all my friendship needs. But I consider my sister Diane to be my prime friend. I'm blessed that this "friend who sticks closer than a [sister]" actually *is* my sister. We talk at least once a week and get together once a year for a longer period.

She knows me and how our family influenced me, and she's seen me over my entire life. I can tell her just about anything at all, and I know she'll listen—carefully and caringly, without judging me—and pray for me.

Jonathan, son of Israel's first king, and David, who would

become Israel's second king, provide a great example of intimate friendship. "After David had finished talking with Saul, Jonathan became one in spirit with David, and he loved him as himself. … And Jonathan made a covenant with David because he loved him as himself" (1 Samuel 18:1, 3). We encourage you to read their story to appreciate the risks they took for one another, the trust they had in each other. They provide a good pattern of friends of the same gender.

Fourth, *develop some intimate relationships with trustworthy mentors.* We always "stand on the shoulders of those who have gone before," especially in relationships. Get to know some solid Christian women who can share the wisdom they've gained over the years. I (Sheila) met Thelma when I was just nineteen years old and thousands of miles from home. Her husband, Herb, led the college/career group I became involved with, and I grew to value her love and her biblical knowledge. I can always trust her to listen, to tell me the truth, and to help me work through my feelings. Although she now lives in another state, she's only a phone call away. I cherish the way she prays for me and my family. She and Herb have been God's gift to me: God with skin on. She taught me by example to help other hurting young women, which I do in a recovery group I'm involved in and as I go about my daily life. I've learned so much from her that I want to share with others.

As Sheila's husband, I (Tim) have one question: Did you notice the second part of Sheila's testimony about the contribution that Thelma has made in her life? Thelma taught Sheila to pass it on to others. That is good advice. Give yourself to some younger women who can benefit from what you've learned. "Likewise, teach the older women to be reverent in the way they live, not to be slanderers or addicted to much wine, but to teach what is good. Then they can train the younger women to love their husbands and children, to be self-controlled and pure, to be busy at home, to be kind, and to be subject to their husbands, so that no one will malign the word of God" (Titus 2:3-5). Mentoring allows you to give to others what has been given to you.

Deepen Marital Intimacy

It is easier to understand the process of building intimacy than to actually do it. We'd like to offer three suggestions that can guide you as a couple as you penetrate to the core of one another. This process may stretch you far beyond your comfort zones, but we can say from experience that the discomfort is well worth the outcome of a deeper, stronger marriage.

First, *spend significant time together.* Sarah's complaint—that she and her husband didn't have anything in common—has much truth in it. Couples do tend to develop different interests and have many different demands on their time. And although they share many activities, they usually don't spend the large amounts of time together as a couple that they did early in their relationship.

Don't hesitate to have lives outside the marriage. Friends, hobbies, and leisure activities all provide needed time away. But don't allow the degree of those pursuits to take away time from your most intimate human relationship. Allow them to complement, not compete with, your marriage.

If you have children, spend good chunks of time together as a family unit. But also spend time with just your spouse. Many marriage experts encourage couples to continue dating, to have one event each week for just the two of them. These activities don't have to blast your budget; fit them into what you can afford.

Second, *talk more.* Remember that wives often spell intimacy c-o-n-v-e-r-s-a-t-i-o-n, while husbands spell it quite differently! This will take some compromise on both your parts!

Wife, don't expect your husband to talk with you as your girlfriends do, and don't try to talk to him as you talk to your girlfriends! Don't dump everything on him and then try to get him to analyze every little detail.

Husband, you'll probably have to significantly increase the amount of time you spend talking with your wife. Wait just a minute; let's reword that statement. Don't *spend* time, *invest* time in conversation. Your time spent should result in a good return of principal for both of you. (We'll explore conversation in more depth in Lie 10.)

Next, *develop common activities so you can spend time with one another.* Intentionally overcome the tendency to have separate lives. Be creative and make these shared activities specific to your lives and interests. Talk about how you can increase your time together in this way.

Many couples get into the same church ministry when their gifts and interests coincide. Joining a couples' Bible study can increase your time together. Husband, as much as you may dislike it, volunteer to go shopping with your wife on occasion. Tim and I (Sheila) have a date night once a week where just the two of us go out to dinner, see a movie, or just take a drive in the country. We live in a valley where sheep and cattle ranchers have homesteaded for a more than a hundred years, and it's fun to watch our little cow town turning into a large city almost overnight. We can get into open country in five minutes, and we often take our convertible out to the coast. A nice drive along the beach and a place to eat will keep me happy for quite a while. I especially like to use this time to talk about some of the issues that have come up in my own life or in our marriage. I know I can always do this on date night over dinner.

You may also share in some common recreational activities, whether it's camping, sports, or hobbies. One couple we know shares a craft hobby. He cuts the wood into the shapes she wants, sands them and puts them together, and then she paints them.

We often enjoy working in the yard together, planting and planning what to go where. We have found out (the hard way!) that we have different ideas on trimming plants, so we've learned to talk about it before we do it!

Another important shared activity that greatly increases intimacy is what most husbands have been impatiently waiting for: sex. Like conversation, this area will likely require compromise for both husbands and wives. Wife, realize that your husband spells intimacy s-e-x. Mutual submission to the other's needs comes into play here, but submission by one does not permit force by the other. We'll examine this subject more thoroughly in Lie 11, but realize that sex both results from intimacy and increases it. Be as free, frequent, and giving as you can in this area.

For building intimacy, you'll do much better when you realize that your spouse sees intimacy a little differently than you do, but you both need it. Commit yourselves to increasing intimacy in your marriage; you'll both benefit. And that's the truth.

Lie 9

Do I Look Good in This Dress? I Really Want to Know

The Truth about Honesty, Criticism, and Affirmation

The men gathered for their weekly accountability group, and the facilitator asked a question to start the talking: "Guys, what do you fear the most and why? Kevin, why don't you begin for us?"

"To be honest, not too many things frighten me. After fighting in the first Gulf War with Special Forces and facing chemical warfare, not much rises to that level. But just last week I got scared almost to death.

"Kelli and I were getting ready to go out to this party for her work, and she tried on a new outfit. Then she turned to me and asked, 'Honey, do you think I look good in this dress?'

"What's a guy to do? I knew I was dead meat. She didn't look real good in it, but she had paid a bundle for it. So, if I say she doesn't look good, then I'm cheap and critical. If I say she does look good, then she gets to the party and some girlfriend tells her the truth, and then I'm in trouble for lying. I let her go to the party looking ugly. I was terrified!"

The rest of the men laughed in sympathy; most had had similar experiences. Kevin's story set the pace for their stories of fear, but none topped his.

The Lie

Did Kelli lie when she simply asked if Kevin liked the dress, assuring him that she really wanted to know? That fits in the category of indirect communication, because on the surface, she literally asked for a fashion critique. In that sense, she told the truth. But below the surface, she wanted Kevin to tell her she looked sexy, that having two children hadn't made her unattractive to him. But she didn't say that, so she didn't communicate the full truth of what she wanted to hear. That's what made her question/statement "Do I look good in this dress? I really want to know" a lie.

Behind the Lie

In our survey for this book, the second most frequent lie mentioned by husbands was "Nothing's wrong; I'm just fine." Wives most often said, "No, this dress isn't new, I've had it for months." But this one about appearance led the men's list.

A complex mixture of factors combines to almost completely bewilder husbands in this area of complimenting and criticizing their wives. Let's explore some of the reasons wives ask their husbands how they look, but want more than a fashion critique.

SENSITIVITY ABOUT THEIR APPEARANCE

Our two grandchildren stayed with us the week we wrote this chapter. Josh had recently turned fourteen, and Hannah was ten. She'd just started horseback riding lessons and needed boots, riding pants, and a shirt. Since the children were with us before the second lesson, she wrangled Grandma into taking her shopping for the proper horse gear. Of course, a few days earlier she'd manipulated Grandpa into taking her on a scouting trip to find the best Western wear stores. Quite a persuasive young lady!

So Grandma took both kids shopping while Grandpa stayed home and worked on the chapter. (Lucky Grandpa!) Hannah found a pair of pants that might do and took them into the dressing room. After a few moments, Grandma called, "Come out and let us see how they look on you."

A voice behind the dressing room door said, "No, not if Joshua is there. I don't want him to see me. He'll laugh."

So, Joshua moved out of sight; only after both Grandma and Hannah had approved of the way she looked was he allowed to come back.

At only ten, Hannah already displayed a typical characteristic of women: sensitivity about appearance. Women derive much of their sense of self-worth and self-image from their appearance. They want their husbands to find them attractive. They want their girlfriends to think they look good. They want to look good for themselves.

This sensitivity about appearance didn't develop just in the modern age. In the New Testament period, some women seemed to have gone overboard in focusing on their physical appearance, enough so that Peter needed to address the issue in his letter. "Your beauty should not come from outward adornment, such as braided hair and the wearing of gold jewelry and fine clothes. Instead, it should be that of your inner self, the unfading beauty of a gentle and quiet spirit, which is of great worth in God's sight" (1 Peter 3:3–4). Peter didn't tell women to avoid outer beauty, but rather to put more emphasis on inner beauty.

Part of the reason, then, that women ask their husbands how they look is that they genuinely want some honest feedback. If a dress makes them look fat, they don't want to wear it out in public. And since their husbands are handy, they ask them how they look in it. So far, there is a pretty simple fashion critique going on. But another factor comes into play as well.

Desire to Be Sexy to Their Husbands

Physical attractiveness makes a significant contribution to a woman's ability to attract a husband. Innately, she wants to please a man with the way she looks. And after she's "caught" him, she continues to want to look good to him. Not only that, she wants to *know* she looks good to him.

We think God created women with this desire, and so did the apostle Paul. That's why he wrote, "But a married woman is concerned about the affairs of this world—how she can please her husband" (1 Corinthians 7:34).

A wife's desire to please her husband expresses a good principle of marriage. By the way, that principle also works in reverse, husband! Looking sexy and being sexy contribute to deepening the bond between a husband and wife. As human beings, God made us physical creatures, endowed with spirit and soul. Each part of our nature influences the other. In the same way, the physical attractiveness of the wife impacts the overall marital closeness in marriage. A husband especially appreciates it when his wife intentionally does things to appear sexy or attractive to him.

Allow us to clarify something here. Wives can dress sexy, or seductively, which emphasizes their sexuality, or they can dress attractively, which emphasizes their physical beauty. Husbands will typically see either as sexually appealing and appreciate it. That's just how they react. But we do encourage wives to keep the seductive stuff at home. Wives must be careful not to add to other men's temptations.

Just as most husbands want their wives to be sexy and attractive, most wives want to know that their husbands view them that way.

On our twenty-fifth anniversary trip to Hawaii, we'd spent one day snorkeling at the beach and came back to take our showers and prepare dinner. Tim noticed that I had put on a wispy sarong, which I had done intentionally. "Ooh, I like that. You're taking my attention off dinner!" We finished dinner and had a nice romantic evening. We both enjoyed my wearing that sarong!

Trouble can come, however, when women combine the desire to be sexy for their husbands with a sensitivity about their appearance.

TENDENCY TO MIX MESSAGES

When a wife says, "Honey, do you think I look good in this

dress?" she may give conflicting messages. One message may be direct; she truly wants a fashion critique. Does the dress she is wearing look good on her? Does it flatter her? Does it fit the occasion? The husband can give some perspective that she appreciates, and she desires his honest opinion.

But she can also give an indirect message, as we mentioned earlier: "Do I look good to you? Am I still sexy despite bearing your children and being ten years older? I want you to tell me that I've still got it."

The problem? A husband usually isn't perceptive enough to tell which message his wife wants him to respond to. If he affirms his wife and tells her that the dress looks perfect on her, even though it doesn't, later when a friend at the party tells her the truth, she gets mad at her husband. Or, if he says the dress doesn't look good on her when she wants affirmation, then he's an insensitive clod who doesn't meet her needs.

When these two factors come together, the result is a conflicted husband and a frustrated wife.

On the Receiving End

Most husbands respond to the question "Do you think I look good in this dress?" the way Kevin did: with fear and dread. They seem instinctively to recognize that their wives may be combining the two factors mentioned above, but they don't quite know how to answer in a way that satisfies both. Does the wife want a fashion critique or an affirmation? Most men don't do subtle very well, and they know that any answer they give may lead them into the danger zone.

So they mumble, "Yeah, honey, you look good in everything," and pray that will keep them out of too much trouble.

Living the Truth

In order to advise husbands about how to answer such loaded questions as "Honey, do you think I look good in this dress?" we need to address several issues that lie at the foundation of such questions. The following discussion, therefore, will be addressed to the wives as well as the husbands.

CHERISH TRUTH

Although both husbands and wives need to cherish truth, wives especially can benefit from it. Wife, when you ask your husband a question such as the one about your appearance, be sure you want an honest, forthright answer from him. Don't use indirect messages, since your husband probably won't pick them up. Men typically respond to the literal meaning of a question, so realize that if you ask for a fashion critique, you'll probably get one.

Also realize that you're asking for your husband's honest opinion. Unless he answers in an obviously rude manner, accept it as such. He risks a lot by telling you the truth as he sees it about your appearance. If you're not really interested in his opinion, don't ask him for it. "That's not what I wanted to hear" won't help him speak up the next time. You can disagree with his opinion, but please don't punish him for giving it. After all, you asked for it.

Try to speak the truth as directly as you can. Men like to fix problems. If you need a fashion critique, make it clear that's what you're asking about. If you need some reassurance that you still look good to him, tell him so directly. Most husbands love to express their opinions to their wives, especially when they know they can do so safely.

Back in 1978 I (Tim) interviewed for a job as associate minister at a church in Lawndale, California. The position involved working directly with the college/career group and overseeing the entire youth ministry. As part of the process, I met with the elders of the church and all the youth sponsors. The beauty of one of the college sponsors stunned me, and I discreetly asked some questions and discovered she was single.

Almost immediately my prayer changed. Before I had prayed, "God, do whatever you want here. I'm okay if I get the job or if I don't get it. Just lead the process." But after I met that young lady I began to pray, "God, please let this work out. I'll accept whatever you do, but I'd really like to get this job." Funny how beauty impacts men!

I did get the job, and the young lady and I began working

together. I discovered that a deep heart for God and a gracious spirit went along with the young woman's physical attractiveness. After five months of watching one another, we began dating. Three months later we got married. This last spring we celebrated twenty-five years of marriage. Obviously, Sheila doesn't look the same as she did then, but her beauty still captivates me, and I enjoy telling her so. She acts a little embarrassed when I do, but I suspect she enjoys it anyway.

I (Sheila) do enjoy it. His compliments make me feel beautiful on the inside even when I think I look ordinary on the outside. About a year ago, we had a wedding to attend for a family friend. I brought several outfits home to get Tim's input, and he said one in particular made me look slender. Over the years, I'd added a few pounds, so slender was good! I kept the outfit, wore it to the wedding, and felt great. His comments made the difference.

Why should you cherish truthful answers? The Bible offers several fascinating responses to that question. This first one links how a person responds to negative information with his basic character. "Do not rebuke a mocker or he will hate you; rebuke a wise man and he will love you" (Proverbs 9:8).

Wife, if you ask for a fashion critique and receive a negative response (this fits into the rebuke category), you can make either a wise response or a foolish response. A wise response is "Thanks for being honest; I do want to look good for this party." A foolish response is "This from the guy who wears a torn T-shirt three days in a row?"

Also, a truthful answer expresses a love that wants and seeks the best. "Better is open rebuke than hidden love. Wounds from a friend can be trusted, but an enemy multiplies kisses" (Proverbs 27:5–6).

When your husband lets you know (graciously), then, that a certain dress doesn't flatter you, even though you paid a lot of money for it and love it, realize that he gave his response out of love. He wants you to look your best. You can avoid a lot of problems in marriage communication if you assume good motives whenever possible.

You see, your husband really does want to help. "A lying tongue hates those it hurts, and a flattering mouth works ruin" (Proverbs 26:28). If you don't look good in the dress, but your husband says you do, then ruin may be on the way! Appreciate his honesty and establish an environment in which he can express the truth as he sees it without receiving grief for it.

SPEAK TRUTH

Husband, this section is primarily for you. Realize that your wife's question, "Honey, do you think I look good in this dress?" may contain two messages. First, "Does this *dress* look good?" Second, "Do *I* look good?" Your survival as a husband depends on how you answer both!

Out of obedience to God and out of love for your wife, we encourage you to answer truthfully. Paul told us in Ephesians 4:15 (NRSV), "But *speaking the truth in love*, we must grow up in every way." Tell your wife the truth about the dress, but don't be brutal. "You know, sweetheart, that dress really does make you look fat, now that you mention it. Oh, you're not fat, but it makes you look that way." That response may be the truth, but speaking the truth in that manner will seal your doom!

Tell her the truth, but do it with love, with grace, and with some respect for her sensitivity about her appearance. "That dress doesn't really bring out your best features." Or, "The other dress emphasizes your slenderness more."

Both of those answers say basically the same thing, but we guarantee they'll be received differently. We assume that you want to benefit your wife, to give an honest appraisal of how she looks in a particular outfit. Just do it in a way that helps her to receive it well, using a method that won't turn you into road kill. No one benefits from that result.

BUILD HER SELF-IMAGE

Husband, when your wife asks you that terrifying, hair-raising question, remember the two messages: "Does this *dress* look good?" and "Do *I* look good?" We suggest that if you regularly affirm the latter, then she'll mean just the former more regularly. Commit to regularly and specifically affirming the physical attractiveness of your wife. Do it with words. Do it with touch. But no matter how you do it, do it frequently. Let her know, without a doubt, that you desire her physically. Don't force her to use indirect statements to drag a compliment about her attractiveness from you. Take the initiative. Overwhelm her with affirmation. Let her know that she still has it.

We read the Song of Songs, also known as the Song of Solomon, in preparing for this chapter. In this collection of lyrical love poems, eight times Solomon praises the physical beauty of his beloved wife. Some expressions are quite graphic, especially in light of the terminology of the times. Some are quite extensive, covering nearly an entire chapter. Here's an excerpt from just one.

> How beautiful are your sandaled feet, O queenly maiden. Your rounded thighs are like jewels, the work of a skilled craftsman. Your navel is as delicious as a goblet filled with wine. Your belly is lovely, like a heap of wheat set about with lilies. Your breasts are like twin fawns of a gazelle. Your neck is as stately as an ivory tower. Your eyes are like the sparkling pools in Heshbon. (Song of Solomon 7:1–4 NLT)

We'll stop there, but this woman's husband goes into even more detail as he praises her beauty. We'll come back to this subject in a later chapter as well, but feel free to read more on your own. Don't steal the compliments of Solomon directly, but get creative with similar statements about the physical attributes of your wife.

Wives do have a great sensitivity about their physical attractiveness. That's why husbands must realize that the simple question, "Honey, do I look good in this dress?" may have a lot more meaning than just a request for a fashion critique. Meet your wife's needs by affirming her attractiveness, and you'll both benefit. And that's the truth.

Lie 10

You Never Talk to Me

The Truth about Conversation

Kent slipped in the door with a sigh, set his briefcase down, and gave Marsha a quick kiss. "How was your day, hon?"

"Oh, typical. I did the 'homeroom mom' bit in the morning for Kari's class, then I put in some laundry. Gosh, those kids sure put out the dirty clothes! I picked up the kids after school, got them started on their homework, and fixed dinner. How was work?"

"Hectic. That Smith-Keller contract has become a little shaky; we have to finesse some of the figures again. I had to bring them home tonight since we present them first thing in the morning. I can help get the kids in bed, but then I need to hit those figures pretty hard."

"Don't be too late coming to bed, okay?"

Kent knocked off the project in about three hours and slid into bed next to a wide-awake Marsha. "Still awake, sweetheart?"

"Yeah, a lot of things have been running through my head. I think we need to talk. Yes, I know now isn't the time. It's late, and we're both tired, but I need to tell you this."

Then she added a good-natured dig. "Besides, if I tell you, then I can get to sleep, and it'll be your turn to toss and turn."

"Thanks, baby, you're so generous. What's on your mind?"

"Kent, we never talk anymore. Oh, we talk, but we don't *talk*. Not about us. We slide over the events of our days, but we don't share much beyond the surface activities. How long has it been since we just sat down, with nothing to do, and talked? Too long. We're both busy, I know, with your new job, the kids and their school activities, and church. I realize it can't be like it was when we were dating. I don't expect that, honest. But you seem so wrapped up in your job. And all you hear from me is the kids, school, and housework. I feel like you just don't care about talking to me. I think we've lost something important to us."

With that, she turned over and soon dropped off. But as Marsha had predicted, Kent tried to process what she had said. He had an MBA, but he couldn't quite figure out why Marsha felt so frustrated. It didn't make sense to him.

The Lie

Despite what many wives like Marsha feel, husbands generally do care about talking to their wives and listening to them. But husbands and wives have very different communication styles, as well as different goals for communication, and different techniques for achieving those goals. Wives often perceive their husbands as not wanting to talk, when in truth, they just don't want to talk the way women talk.

So when wives tell their husbands, as Marsha did, "You never talk to me," whether they realize it or not, that is a lie.

Behind the Lie

Radically different styles of communication lead to tremendous conflict and frustration between husbands and wives. Understanding the differences will provide a clue as to why wives think their husbands don't care about talking to them.

WOMEN ARE MORE VERBAL

Tim once attended a Promise Keepers rally where the

speaker said that men average thirty thousand words per day, and women average fifty thousand, as he best recalls. That seems accurate and flows directly from differences between male and female brains.

Some time ago, doctors noticed that women stroke victims recovered much more fully than men, and so the doctors sought to discover the reason. They learned that women tend to use both sides of the brain while speaking, and men tend to use just one hemisphere. So when a stroke occurs, the unaffected part of the female brain is able to pick up communication tasks more easily since it has been doing some of that work already. Some studies suggest that female brains have more connections between the hemispheres than do male brains.

As we discussed in a previous chapter, women tend to speak indirectly more than men. This tendency may come from their greater overall ability to read nonverbal cues, such as body posture and movement, tone of voice, facial expressions, eye contact, use of space, and touch. Each of these carries meaning that can add to the actual words.

In one of his video series, Dr. James Dobson encouraged viewers to watch young children at play, at an age before they are taught how boys and girls should act. When together, girls typically talk and role play. Boys typically play games and make a variety of sounds like grunts and explosions. Those differences continue into adulthood.

Women tend to use conversation to examine an issue from various perspectives and process through it, while men tend to use conversation to discover how to fix a problem or reach a goal. "Let's cut to the chase" is a typical male phrase, meaning, "Let's skip all the unnecessary stuff; what do we need to know to do the right thing and get the desired result?"

THE ROAD TO INTIMACY

Women tend to view conversation as the road to intimacy, while men view conversation as the road to a solution.

Deborah Tannen, in a 1995 study, suggested that females use communication to negotiate closeness, or intimacy, while males use communication to negotiate status, or competition.[1]

As quoted by Deborah Tannen, Dr. Cynthia Torppa of Ohio State University said, "Women tend to be relationship specialists and men tend to be task specialists."[2] In her book *You Just Don't Understand*, Tannen said that women use "rapport talk": they use compliments and personal touches to build the relationship. Men tend to use "report talk": they share facts and playful insults.[3]

These findings help reveal why men and women have such different approaches to conversation: they have different goals. An hour of just sitting together and talking about "stuff" builds intimacy in women, but it feels like conversation overkill to many men.

WOMEN LISTEN DIFFERENTLY

The following observations are taken from the previously cited book by Tannen, along with another of her books, *Talking from 9 to 5*.[4] Keep in mind that these are general tendencies; you'll always find exceptions.

> Men tend to avoid prolonged direct eye contact because they typically interpret it as either confrontational if done by a male or flirty if done by a female. Even if they don't look at the conversation partner, they still listen. Women, however, use more direct eye contact to help keep the focus on the conversation, and they tend to interpret the absence or avoidance of eye contact as not listening.
>
> The genders also deal with opposing ideas differently. Men will often play "devil's advocate" and bring up ideas they don't necessarily agree with in order to explore possibilities. They don't intend to challenge the other person; they merely want to look at the topic in greater detail. Women often view

opposing ideas as a personal attack on them
or their ideas.

With all of these differences in mind, it is easy to see why
Marsha thought Kent just didn't care about talking to her.

On the Receiving End

Kent did care. He appreciated the way he and Marsha
touched base with one another every day when he got home.
They had family discussions at the dinner table. He liked
talking to her, but he did struggle with *how* they talked. "Why
does she have to talk about everything, over and over? Can't
she just get to the subject? She beats around the bush before
she gets to the topic. Then she talks all around it before getting
to the point."

Dr. Laura Schlessinger, in her book *The Proper Care and
Feeding of Husbands*, suggests that wives want to converse
with their husbands like the wives do with their girlfriends: to
show interest and to agree uncritically. Husbands think their
wives tell them stuff so they can do something about it. Neither
is wrong, except they both expect the wrong conversation.
Neither can fully meet the conversational expectations of the
other.

Schlessinger encourages women to communicate less
in order to communicate better,[5] and Kent could identify
with that suggestion. He felt overwhelmed with all the
talking Marsha wanted to do, and any less discussion just
frustrated her.

Without knowing why, Kent felt a little bit like Marsha
was playing basketball and he was playing chess: they operated
with different rules and goals. He couldn't identify just what
the differences were, but he knew they didn't quite connect
when they did talk. Marsha didn't think they talked enough,
and he thought they talked too much. Basically, he felt overwhelmed and bewildered.

Living the Truth

Developing good conversation between a husband and

wife takes a great deal of work and compromise by both. And although every couple will implement them differently, the following suggestions can provide the foundation for mutually satisfying conversation.

GIVE A LITTLE

Skilled communicators adjust how they speak so the listener can best and most easily understand. We each need the same "audience orientation" that Paul had when he spoke. He had a passion to reach people, and he spoke in terms that his audience could understand the best.

> To the Jews I became like a Jew, to win the Jews. To those under the law I became like one under the law ... so as to win those under the law. To those not having the law I became like one not having the law ... so as to win those not having the law. To the weak I became weak, to win the weak. I have become all things to all men so that by all possible means I might save some. (1 Corinthians 9:20–22)

Wife, if you want to have a satisfying talk with your husband, then adjust a little so he can relate. Don't expect him to talk like a woman, and try to decrease the amount of what you share. Focus on what's most important to you. If he doesn't look deeply into your eyes the whole time, realize that he is still listening. And if he brings up opposing ideas, don't assume that he disagrees with you. It's just how he thinks.

Husband, if you want to meet the conversational needs of your wife, realize that she views talking as the road to intimacy. She wants to hear the details of your life. Spend more time than you feel comfortable with in talking to her. Mostly, try to understand the vital role that communication plays for her.

BUILD IN TIME FOR CONVERSATION

Talking more to their wives can really frighten some men, so we suggest you consider scheduling a regular time for just the two of you to talk. Otherwise, you can conveniently forget to do it until it builds into a crisis.

I (Tim) remember that when Dad came home from work each day, he and Mom would sit at the kitchen table over a cup of coffee and talk about their day. They didn't exclude my sister and me, but we had little interest in those grown-up conversations and pretty much left the two of them alone. Looking back, I believe that those conversations made up a large part of their strong bond with each other.

Every couple will do this differently, but please do it. Have a regular time together to talk.

DEVELOP LISTENING SKILLS

The best single listening skill husbands can develop is the ability just to listen, to neither lecture nor try to fix. God wired men as "report talkers," and they like to fix things. So they listen for the facts and propose solutions. But they accommodate best when they realize that their wives just need to talk sometimes. Wives don't need or want someone telling them what to do. They just want undivided attention from their husbands. And conversation involves give and take, so participate. Share your thoughts and feelings, but don't dominate.

The best single listening skill wives can develop is the ability not to confuse listening with agreement. Tim has sometimes counseled couples with marriage problems, and frequently the wife has complained about her husband, saying, "He just doesn't hear me." But as Tim has probed, he has often found that the husband had heard very accurately. He just didn't agree with her. She thought that if he had truly heard her, he would have agreed. Wife, be content if your husband understands what you say. Believe us, if he does, you're well ahead of the game!

Now, let's look at some specific listening skills that both husbands and wives can use to enhance their conversation. Joseph DeVito, in his book *Human Communication,* lists eight factors of effective listening.[6] Each matched pair represents the opposite end of a continuum. Each skill has an appropriate use and an appropriate time. Learning to understand when to focus on which skill will improve your listening.

Empathic and objective listening deal with the tension between listening to understand what a person feels and objective reality. You listen empathically as you try to understand the speaker's point of view. You don't have to agree, but you want to see it as the other person sees it. You listen objectively as you match what the individual says with reality. Kent could have used empathic listening if he'd tried to get inside Marsha's head, to learn why she felt frustrated at their level of conversation. He could have listened objectively as he evaluated how often they talk about personal issues now versus how often they did earlier.

Nonjudgmental and critical listening involve knowing the proper time to evaluate what you hear. We encourage you to first listen nonjudgmentally, to focus on understanding what your spouse says. Don't focus on what matches reality, just try to comprehend what is being said. Then listen critically, make an evaluation. Is the speaker correct? Partially correct? Until you understand the message, you really can't evaluate it.

Surface and depth listening look for the multiple layers of meaning. You hear the surface meaning when you listen literally to the obvious meaning of the words. But most messages have more than just a surface meaning, and that deeper message may even contradict the surface message. A previous lie—"Nothing's wrong; I'm just fine"—explored indirect messages. On the surface, the wife was saying she was fine. In truth, she was not fine. Depth listening focuses on the indirect message underneath the surface. Husbands tend to listen more literally and thus don't pick up on depth messages as well as their wives do.

When Marsha said, "You don't care about talking to me anymore," Kent immediately started counting up the times they did talk: when he got home from work, at the dinner table, in bed. He responded to the surface message and couldn't understand why his wife felt so frustrated.

But Marsha included some depth messages as well. She communicated frustration. She communicated a lack of intimacy with her husband, the fact that their lives didn't connect enough. She communicated a fear that she didn't play a vital enough role in his life. But he missed those messages.

Active and inactive listening deal with the level of interaction by the listener. Inactive listening responds with "Yes," or "Oh really?" or other expressions that merely let the speaker know the listener hasn't fallen asleep. Husbands frequently do this. And for both genders, not responding to a statement that will merely increase conflict with no possible resolution can be a wise choice.

Active listening, however, probes for the full meaning. You listen actively when you paraphrase the speaker's meaning back to him or her in your words. You strive to understand his or her feelings. You ask probing questions. You try to clarify what he or she meant—the implications—to take the topic a little deeper.

Although Kent didn't have a chance to reword Marsha's meaning that night, if he had done so the next day, he would have both surprised and pleased her. Active listening tells the speaker that you care about her—her thoughts and feelings—and that you want to connect with her in communication.

Of all these listening skills, active listening may do more than any other single skill to enhance your ability to connect with your spouse. But some general skills of conversational competence will greatly increase your ability to converse in a mutually satisfying manner.

BUILD CONVERSATIONAL COMPETENCE

DeVito explores seven skills of conversational competence.[7] We've already covered some of them, but three have great importance for communication by couples.

Openness begins with both parties sharing information about themselves—their feelings, thoughts, struggles, and joys.

Husband, you probably can't begin to imagine the details of your life that your wife would love to know. We realize that men struggle with self-disclosure, but remember that wives spell intimacy c-o-n-v-e-r-s-a-t-i-o-n, and conversation requires talk, so as you open yourself to her, you'll increase the relational intimacy, which can also increase the physical intimacy. Not a bad trade-off.

Openness also involves being genuinely willing to listen to the messages from your spouse and to react to them. To put it another way, try to understand what she says, and don't ignore it.

Kent could have used openness by asking Marsha some questions about why she felt as she did, along with sharing his thoughts and feelings about how much they talked. If you use this conversational skill, try to avoid getting defensive, but honestly express yourself.

Positiveness means caring about the other person and the relationship and making it clear that you value both. Wife, make an effort to build up your husband, as we've discussed before. Avoid having a critical attitude, seeing problems in everything. Avoid having a negative attitude, opposing whatever he says almost as a matter of principle.

How you phrase statements can express positiveness. Husband, if your wife asks if you like a certain dress and you know it makes her look fat, you can respond negatively by saying, "Gosh, you look like two pounds of sausage stuffed in a one-pound casing," or you can positively say, "You know, I think that gray dress brings out the color of your eyes better." With both statements, you encourage her to wear something else, but she'll appreciate the latter! (And you'll live longer!)

Positiveness also involves "stroking" the other person, letting your spouse know that he or she and the relationship between the two of you are important to you. Nice comments about your spouse, a smile, or a hug all communicate that positive message.

The next day, Kent could have used a positive approach to let Marsha know that he did care about her and the conversation. He could have come home from work, held her in his arms, and said, "You know, I've been doing a lot of thinking about what you said last night. I'm glad you told me how you feel, I really am. I want our marriage to satisfy both of us. Let's talk about how we can find more time just to talk."

Immediacy involves linking with the other person, thus creating a sense of togetherness. Immediacy indicates that you care about your spouse and the encounter. How do you build a sense of intimacy? By making appropriate eye contact and avoiding looking away. Wife, if you want immediacy in a conversation with your husband, don't begin it when he's watching his favorite football team in a big game. Husband, don't start an important conversation while your wife's cooking dinner.

Physical closeness also plays a large role in effective conversation. In several of the very difficult discussions we've had as a couple, we have sat next to each other on a love seat. Although some of our emotions have seemed to urge us to get as far from the other as possible, we have both wanted to communicate to one another that we're together and need to work out things between us. In the scenario we just mentioned, Kent's taking Marsha in his arms and speaking positively to her would have enhanced immediacy between them.

Truly, a mutually satisfying conversational life between a husband and wife can seem impossible at times. As we have noted, men and women communicate in such different ways that true conversation between them is often difficult. But we encourage both of you to respond to the conversation needs of your mate. Learn to be more flexible, more understanding, more willing to conform to the conversational needs of your partner. Use this chapter as a guide, and you will improve your conversations. And that's the truth.

Lie 11

Not Tonight, Dear; I Have a Headache

The Truth about Sexual Intimacy

Jerry and Barb helped the kids with their homework after dinner, then they watched a little TV before putting the kids to bed. He graded some papers for class the next day as Barb worked on paying the bills. He finished his work, gave her a lingering kiss, and said, "I'm heading for bed. You about ready?"

Barb recognized the signs and smothered her sense of dread. She smiled and replied, "Yeah, I hope so. I need to finish this though."

"Okay, I'll be waiting." And with another kiss, he headed to the bedroom.

Jerry showered, shaved, and turned down the bedding. Still no Barb. After half an hour of reading, he walked back to the family room where she sat with the bills spread out before her. She noticed he had just his pajama bottoms on—another clear sign of what he anticipated.

"Hey, you're taking a long time. I hoped we could get some time to make love. Seems like it's been a while."

"Not tonight, dear; I have a headache. Must be from working on these bills, and I still have a few to pay. Maybe tomorrow?"

"Yeah, sure. And tomorrow never arrives. I know that

story," he mumbled as he went back to bed—alone—and Barb stayed up another hour or so.

The Lie

Barb didn't have a headache, although she did feel tired. And she'd finished the bills. In truth, she didn't want to make love to Jerry, so she used both the bills and the headache as excuses. For women like Barb who struggle with responding sexually to their husbands, a variety of factors combine to make them hesitant in this area. Nevertheless, their husbands perceive their hesitancy as a personal rejection.

On the Receiving End

Sexual rejection strikes at the very core of a man. In their book 5 *Love Needs of Men and Women*, Dr. Gary and Barbara Rosberg say that between 50 and 90 percent of a man's self-image comes from his sexuality.[1] So when a man's wife rejects having sex with him, in his mind she rejects him. Men tend to link the two. A single rejection won't carry too much weight, but repeated rebuffs are cumulative in their impact.

In previous chapters we looked at how wives spell intimacy c-o-n-v-e-r-s-a-t-i-o-n, while men spell intimacy s-e-x. Men don't see sex as just physical, but as a way to intimately connect with their wives. Sexual rejection weakens the very marital bond.

That rejection typically results in men feeling emasculated. When their main source of masculine identity is denied, it affects men deeply. Their self-confidence becomes threatened. That rejection can lead to anger in husbands, an anger that touches more than just issues relating to sex.

Men do tend to have high sexual needs, and when their wives reject them, that rejection increases the temptations they face. Please don't take us wrong; nothing excuses going outside of marriage for sexual fulfillment. But the temptation level will increase when wives don't meet the sexual needs of their husbands.

When their marriage doesn't meet a prime need, men tend to withdraw from the relationship. Because of how much they risk with rejection, they can shut their wives out of their emotional lives.

So why would women do something that has such a negative impact on their husbands?

Behind the Lie

There are a variety of reasons why many women resist sexual involvement with their husbands. Every couple who experiences sexual tension may have a unique blend of such reasons, but the following represent some of the major causes.

PHYSICAL CONDITIONS

Wives have a lot on their plates today, especially if they have children at home or if they work outside the home. Wives often struggle to respond sexually when they feel tired and run down. When a wife claims to have a headache, she may be telling the truth, at least in part.

A variety of physical conditions can affect wives' sexual desire. For some women, sexual intercourse can result in a significant amount of pain. Hormone levels can affect responsiveness. Medication can also influence the degree of desire and the ability to achieve an orgasm. We encourage all wives who don't enjoy sex, or who resist it, to check with their physicians to see if they might have some physical reason for doing so. Sometimes, a change in medication can make all the difference in the world.

LACK OF SEXUAL ENJOYMENT

Forty years ago, many people, including many ministers and even medical and mental health experts, thought women just didn't enjoy sex at all. It was commonly accepted that most wives carried out their "marital duty" as an obligation, not a pleasure. In some areas of the upper Midwest, women would hide the fact of their pregnancy as long as they could. Why? Pregnancy was seen as evidence that they "did it," and decent women pretended that such "vulgar activity" didn't happen in their lives.

The sexual revolution of the 1960s destroyed that myth and allowed women to accept and admit their sexuality. But that wasn't anything new. Listen to Paul's advice, written nearly two thousand years ago: "The husband should not deprive his wife of sexual intimacy, which is her right as a married woman, nor should the wife deprive her husband" (1 Corinthians 7:3 NLT). Paul recognized that both men and women have sexual needs. And notice that he first told the men to meet the sexual needs of their wives, not vice versa! Although single, Paul understood at least something about women.

But some women—and for a number of reasons—get little pleasure from sex and therefore avoid it. If a previous bad experience with sex has caused this aversion, or if it is the result of sexual abuse, we encourage wives to see a good counselor and work through these issues. Not just to increase the sexual pleasure in their marriage, but to decrease the number of unresolved issues that bring pain to their life. We encourage them to take some time to examine why they don't derive enjoyment in this area that plays such an important role in developing intimacy in marriage.

UNMET INTIMACY NEEDS

Because women focus so much on relationship issues, when their husbands don't meet their overall intimacy needs, they find it difficult to respond sexually. This situation represents what we think is the major reason many wives resist sex. They don't feel that their husbands care for them, so why should they care for their husbands?

That was Barb's main reason. She felt somewhat isolated from Jerry. Their busy lives kept them from talking very much with just the two of them, and the kids seemed to prevent very much marital "dating." To Barb, the only way Jerry wanted to connect with her was sexually, and she felt used. Emotionally she felt drained and unvalued; as a result, she just didn't have very much to give to him in this area.

Jerry didn't treat her in a mean or cruel manner; he just didn't do much to fill her emotional tank. He was a good provider, a nice man, a solid Christian, but emotionally his wife had simply run dry.

ONGOING POWER STRUGGLES

Instead of the marriage in which each spouse submits to the needs of the other, which we discussed earlier, too many marriages slip into a power struggle. Both partners use the tools they have to exert their will on the other, and many wives have discovered that granting or withholding sex often results in their getting their way. Typically having a stronger sex drive, and being more easily aroused, men have a particular vulnerability—and thus a distinct weakness—in this area.

When Randy and Peggy got in a fight, and if Peggy didn't win, she'd stop all sex for months at a time. She made her husband pay for having won. He still attended college, and there were a lot of attractive and friendly girls in his classes. So the longer the involuntary abstinence lasted, the more attractive those young ladies became. He never strayed, but he did struggle. Randy and Peggy were married five years before they finally broke up, but their intimacy was broken long before their marriage ended.

Living the Truth

Probably nothing short of a relationship with God has more power in a marriage than does sex. But unlike knowing God, the power of sex can be used either to build solid intimacy or to cause tremendous damage. Let's explore what God designed sex to be and how it can be maximized in marriage. We'll break this section into three parts: what both the husband and the wife can do, what the husband can do, and what the wife can do.

BOTH HUSBAND AND WIFE: CELEBRATE SEXUALITY

God gave us a tremendous gift when he designed sex in marriage. He desired sex to serve as perhaps the primary tool to build an intimate connection between a husband and wife. Listen to God's blueprint for marriage, as described in his Word:

> For this reason a man will leave his father and mother and be united to his wife, and they will become one flesh. The man and his wife were both naked, and they felt no shame. (Genesis 2:24-25)

What tremendous statements of intimacy! An intimacy that touches the unique needs of both men and women. Spouses leave parents to make the marriage their primary human relationship. When done right, doesn't that give the wife a sense of security and the husband a sense of being valued? They unite in a union stronger at its best than any other human relationship. That kind of relationship provides a solid base for intimacy.

Husband and wife become one flesh, as they unite their bodies physically. They are naked, meaning that they make themselves vulnerable and attractive to one another. They feel no shame, affirming that this style of intimacy is good and God-ordained.

God encourages married couples to engage in sex freely, frequently, and sacrificially. He wants them to strive for mutual satisfaction.

> The husband should not deprive his wife of sexual intimacy, which is her right as a married woman, nor should the wife deprive her husband. The wife gives authority over her body to her husband, and the husband also gives authority over his body to his wife. So do not deprive each other of sexual relations. The only exception to this rule would be the agreement of both husband and wife to refrain from sexual intimacy for a limited time, so they can give themselves more completely to prayer. Afterward they should

come together again so that Satan won't be able to tempt them because of their lack of self-control. (1 Corinthians 7:3–5 NLT)

The goal: a great sex life that satisfies both husband and wife. A sex life in which each partner puts the other first, before self. Both partners have sexual desires, and both have intimacy needs. God designed marriage as the vehicle to satisfy those desires and fulfill those needs.

And for married couples, he doesn't forbid very much. In Scripture, we've found only three categories of acts that have no place in marriage. First, God forbids intercourse or any sexual activity with anyone other than one's husband or wife (1 Corinthians 6:18). This thus excludes sexual activity before marriage, adultery, incest, homosexuality, and orgies. Second, God forbids bestiality, not a major concern for most married couples (Exodus 22:19). Third, he forbids anything that offends the conscience of either partner (Romans 14:23).

In Romans 14 Paul wrote about the issue of eating meat that had been sacrificed to idols. In so doing, he provided a scriptural principle that applies here in the area of sexual relations.

> Accept Christians who are weak in faith, and don't argue with them about what they think is right or wrong. For instance, one person believes it is all right to eat anything. But another believer who has a sensitive conscience will eat only vegetables. Those who think it is all right to eat anything must not look down on those who won't. And those who won't eat certain foods must not condemn those who do, for God has accepted them. ... But if people have doubts about whether they should eat something, they shouldn't eat it. They would be condemned for not acting in faith before God. If you do

anything you believe is not right, you are sinning. (Romans 14:1–3, 23 NLT)

So, if one partner thinks a particular act is wrong, or even just distasteful, then the other partner should submit to the spouse's desire not to engage in it. However, the "weaker" partner would show great love by exploring why he or she disapproves of the act or dislikes it, perhaps even getting with a counselor to work through the issue. But the key is mutually submitting to the other as the path to a satisfying sex life together.

We hope you see a glimpse of the joy that God wants couples to experience in sex. We'll touch on this subject a little more as we explore the Song of Songs. But please don't page ahead to that place; stay on track.

BOTH HUSBAND AND WIFE: STUDY YOUR PARTNER

As we've often said before, every couple is unique. Every person has different desires, drives, pleasures, and hesitations. So if you truly desire to please your spouse in the sexual area, you need to know your partner: deeply, intimately, and accurately. So, here's your homework assignment.

Talk to your spouse. Ask them what they like, and what they don't like. Try to discover why. What frequency do they feel comfortable with? What level of adventurousness will they explore? What excites them? What do they find offensive or repulsive?

We realize that for some couples, frank talk about sexual needs and desires may be uncomfortable. But remember God's design of being naked and unashamed. God created us with sexual desires, and he gave us marriage to meet them. Sex is good and holy when done right, and knowing how to please one another helps make it more right.

Observe your spouse. Discover what works, what doesn't, and when and why. And realize that no one is always consistent. A spouse may find that one sex act is pleasing and satisfying to the other partner at one time but not at another time. We have no clue as to why that happens, but we think it's good; it tends to keep partners from getting in a rut.

HUSBAND: TALK, TALK, AND TALK SOME MORE

Husband, we know you spell intimacy s-e-x, but your wife spells it c-o-n-v-e-r-s-a-t-i-o-n or t-a-l-k. So, if you want your form of intimacy, give her form to her. Meet her intimacy needs; fill up her emotional tank so it can spill over into the bedroom. We've discussed several ways to do this in previous chapters, and we won't repeat ourselves. But if you want great sex, meet your wife's emotional needs.

Here are a few tips that we haven't *touched* on yet. (Pardon the play on words, but it was intentional.) Many wives complain that their husbands never touch them unless they want to end up in the bedroom, and that complaint has a lot of validity. Wives value nonsexual touching, as Sheila has told Tim on more than one occasion!

Husband, touch your wife, frequently. Talk with her about what physical expressions of affection mean the most to her. Here are some possibilities. Hold her hand as you walk, the way you did before you got married. Hug her frequently. While she's cooking dinner, come up from behind her (let her know you're there; don't startle her) and put your arms around her. If you sit next to one another at a restaurant, put your arm on her shoulder. You may want to give a little squeeze so she realizes what you are doing. Give her a kiss just before you leave for work, when you return, and before you turn over in bed to go to sleep. Helping out around the house or with the kids will also communicate to her that your care about her.

Be creative! Before you married her, you probably loved to touch her any time you were able. That sign of affection helped win her heart. Keep it up, to keep her heart warm to you.

HUSBAND: BE SCRUPULOUSLY FAITHFUL

Husband, your wife will find it extremely difficult to express her sexuality to you if you don't convince her of your faithfulness. When I (Tim) got caught up in viewing soft-core porn on the Internet several years ago, it nearly destroyed our marriage. And it did prevent any touching for a long time. I still grieve over the pain I brought Sheila by that foolish act of emotional infidelity.

Your wife needs to know that you view her as your "one and only" in every way. Didn't you pledge to do so in your wedding vows? Faithfulness gives wives the security to risk by fully giving themselves sexually to their husbands. Otherwise, they feel used and vulnerable.

Several bible passages support and clarify that fact. For example, "Marriage should be honored by all, and the marriage bed kept pure, for God will judge the adulterer and all the sexually immoral" (Hebrews 13:4). Purity in marriage means that nothing exists in the sexual lives and thoughts of a couple that doesn't belong there. Obviously, touching another person in an inappropriate manner is totally unacceptable behavior for a marriage partner. Keep sexual actions between you and your mate.

But marital fidelity goes deeper than refraining from outward sexual acts. Many husbands and wives fantasize about previous or imaginary lovers. Many husbands, and even some wives, look at other people or their images in ways that don't belong in marriage. This kind of unfaithful activity can involve looking at real-life people or at images from magazines, on television or the Internet, or in books. Whatever its source, it doesn't belong in marriage. Jesus made that point clear: "You have heard that it was said, 'Do not commit adultery.' But I tell you that anyone who looks at a woman lustfully has already committed adultery with her in his heart" (Matthew 5:27-28).

Husband, you bear the responsibility of showing your wife that you can and will act in a scrupulously faithful manner. As you do so, you will give her the security to give herself to you. That's a nice exchange.

WIFE: UNDERSTAND MASCULINE INTIMACY

Wives often view their husbands as sex-crazed animals

whom they can never satisfy and who never think of anything else but sex. As a man, I (Tim) believe those descriptions have a lot of truth in them! Sex thoughts run through the masculine mind with sometimes distressing regularity. Men typically do have a strong sex drive. And just as feminine hormones affect women with their monthly menstrual cycle, so masculine hormones affect men—but much more frequently than once a month, more like once a minute!

Wife, if that fact bothers you, and it very well may, realize that God designed men this way. So take that issue up with God, not with your husband. But we encourage you to change how you interpret his sex drive. He doesn't just desire physical release. He desires intimate connection with you. That realization should put his constant desire for sex in a totally different light.

A husband named Herb made this comment in Schlessinger's book: "My wonderful wife has put it best: 'Sex is to a husband what conversation is to a wife. When a wife deprives her husband of sex for days, even weeks on end, it is tantamount to his refusing to talk to her for days, even weeks.'"[2] Doesn't that sound like the intimacy you crave, but in a different way?

For a man, sex provides the primary way of connecting with his wife in an intimate way. Most men aren't good at intimate conversation and romantic touches, but they express their need for communion when they join their wife physically. That physical bond creates a strong emotional bond in a man, which then allows him to give himself to her in the emotional ways she needs.

But all this change in a husband's attitude and behavior begins with a change in the way his wife interprets his desire for sex. One wife phrased it like this: "I've quit saying, 'All my husband wants to do is have sex with me.' Now I think, 'All my husband wants to do is to be close to me.' That's totally changed how I look at our sex life!"

Now, let's explore how you can meet your husband's need for sexual intimacy.

WIFE: CAPTIVATE YOUR HUSBAND

We spent a lot of time thinking of how to title this section, and thanks to Roget's Thesaurus we came up with what we think may be the perfect word: *captivate*. You see, wife, when you meet your husband's needs for intimacy through meeting his sexual needs, you capture him: heart, soul, mind, and body. We believe that if you will do so, you will experience benefits that you could never have imagined.

We'll explore four principles from the Song of Songs that can teach you how to utterly captivate your husband. This book contains conversations between the Lover, usually identified with Solomon, and the Beloved, often thought of as his new wife. If you'd like to explore this subject further, we suggest reading *Solomon on Sex*, by Joseph Dillow. It's an older book and hard to find, but well worth it.[3]

1. Enjoy sensuality and attractiveness. Wife, you have a great example in the Beloved of how to enjoy sensuality and your own beauty. You don't have to be ashamed of the feminine beauty with which God has graced you. "Dark am I, yet lovely, O daughters of Jerusalem, dark like the tents of Kedar, like the tent curtains of Solomon" (1:5). "I am a rose of Sharon, a lily of the valleys" (2:1). The Beloved was not ashamed of thinking she looked good—especially to her lover.

Many wives complain because their husbands quit wooing them once they got married, even as they themselves didn't keep themselves as attractive as they had been before. Allow inner godliness to be your primary beauty, as we saw in 1 Peter 3:3-4, but do pay attention to your appearance, your behavior, your conversation and attitude. Feel free to wisely maintain and enhance all these God-given attractions!

Also, enjoy the body and beauty of your husband, and tell him and others that you do! Six times in the book of Solomon, the Beloved expresses her appreciation and enjoyment of her lover's appearance. We think the following passage is the best example. In verse 9 of chapter 5, friends ask the Beloved what is so special about her lover. She then begins to tell them:

My lover is radiant and ruddy, outstanding among ten thousand. His head is purest gold; his hair is wavy and black as a raven. His eyes are like doves by the water streams, washed in milk, mounted like jewels. His cheeks are like beds of spice yielding perfume. His lips are like lilies dripping with myrrh. His arms are rods of gold set with chrysolite. His body is like polished ivory decorated with sapphires. His legs are pillars of marble set on bases of pure gold. His appearance is like Lebanon, choice as its cedars. His mouth is sweetness itself; he is altogether lovely. This is my lover, this my friend, O daughters of Jerusalem. (Song of Songs 5:10-16)

But the Beloved realizes that romance isn't just a spectator sport. In this account, six times the Lover initiates sexual activity, and she does so more than twice as much: fourteen times. She begins the book with inviting him to kiss her: "Let him kiss me with the kisses of his mouth—for your love is more delightful than wine" (1:2).

She asks him to embrace and arouse her: "His left arm is under my head, and his right arm embraces me" (2:6). That sounds okay, but nothing special. Until you realize that the Hebrew word for *embrace* can mean "to fondle or titillate."[4] That sounds like much more than just a hug, doesn't it?

She uses the term *lilies* in reference to her breasts, which she asks him to kiss: "My lover is mine and I am his; he browses among the lilies" (2:16).

Just one more example. The next paragraph accurately conveys the meaning of the symbols used in the original language, and it matches what several commentators say, particularly Dillow in *Solomon on Sex*. We'd like you to know, however, that the symbols can get quite explicit, so feel free to skip the following paragraph if you think it might make you uncomfortable.

Typically, the term *garden* refers to the female genitals,

and some commentators believe the *north wind* and the *south wind* refer to a variety of caresses. With that in mind, read this verse: "Awake, north wind, and come, south wind! Blow on my garden, that its fragrance may spread abroad. Let my lover come into his garden and taste its choice fruits" (4:16). That verse could be paraphrased, "Caress me until I'm aroused and then taste me."

The entire book reveals a godly woman who appreciates sexual enjoyment with her husband. Wife, the more joy you take in sex, the more joy your husband will take in his relationship with you.

2. Teach him how to love you. In our earlier examination of a common misconception, we stated that most wives wish their husbands understood them enough that they didn't have to tell them what to do. Please don't make that mistake with your husband in this context. With their primarily visual stimulation, men need to learn how their wives can best enjoy romance. That will differ for each wife, so like the Beloved in the verses we read above, you will need to teach your husband what you like and what you don't like, what "turns you on" and what "turns you off."

3. Take the initiative. Many husbands say that few things tell them more clearly that their wives enjoy sex than their initiation of the process. The Beloved understood that fact; she initiated sexual activity more than twice as much as her husband. If you don't really know how to initiate sexual relations with your husband, here are a couple of suggestions to get you started. Give him a call at work and tell him you're waiting for him, all alone. Schedule a special date, get a babysitter for the kids, and reserve a room at a local hotel. Use your imagination to come up with other ways to surprise and delight him.

We don't suggest that you start things two-thirds of the time, as the Beloved did, but do respond to your husband's sexual needs for intimacy by taking the lead every so often. That doesn't necessarily mean you'll increase the frequency of lovemaking, just that you will initiate it more often.

4. Be adventurous. Men sometimes get stuck in a rut by doing pretty much the same thing again and again. That lack of variety and spontaneity can get boring, so be adventurous, like the Beloved. "Come, my lover, let us go to the countryside, let us spend the night in the villages. Let us go early to the vineyards to see if the vines have budded, if their blossoms have opened, and if the pomegranates are in bloom—there I will give you my love" (7:11–12).

Go beyond the comfort zone of what you typically do. Be creative in ways that can freshen and reinvigorate your lovemaking with one another.

We understand that wives often think their husbands are sex-crazed animals whom they'll never be able to satisfy. If that is the way you view your husband, remind yourself that s-e-x is how men spell intimacy. Make the effort to build sexual intimacy with your husband, and both of you will benefit. And that's the truth.

Lie 12

You Need to Grow Up and Face Responsibility

The Truth about Adventure

Every year Chad, Crystal, Nick, and Misti would rent a small house in Mt. Shasta, California, for a week and enjoy the mountains. They'd met as couples back in college and had stayed close over the intervening decade. On this year's trip the guys spent the day fishing on the upper Sacramento River, a beautiful stream about twenty yards wide, and the girls hit some of the antique shops in the old railroad town of Dunsmuir.

That night they gathered around the barbecue grill on the patio and sipped iced tea. "So guys, how'd you do with the fishing?" Misti asked. "Catch any trout?"

Nick grinned and said, "Yeah, we got some nice ones. Chad pulled in a real big eighteen-inch rainbow. He had to finesse him fifty yards downstream to pull him in. But that wasn't the show of the day."

Chad interrupted. "Come on, now, dude, you don't have to bore the girls with this." He feared the consequences if this story came out, but Nick pressed on, oblivious to Chad's mounting discomfort.

"No, no, no, this story of courage and physical dexterity begs to be told! Get this, we're fishing downstream, and we spot this gorgeous pool. Probably ten feet deep, but we can't get to it. This huge twenty-foot-tall boulder blocks our access to the top of the pool, and then another boulder the same size blocks the tail end. But mountain man Chad starts poking around, finds a crack between those two big rocks, climbs up there, and I see him, twenty feet in the air, halfway perched on a small pine tree growing out of the rock.

"He drops his line in, and I don't know how in the world he could have pulled one in if he'd hooked it. But what courage! He could have hurt himself bad if he'd fallen. But old Chad fished the hole. Too bad he never got a bite!"

Later, in their bedroom, Crystal unloaded. "Chad, I can't believe you did that. Climbing that huge rock and hanging onto a small tree. You're not a footloose college kid anymore. You're thirty years old; you have a wife, a job, and a child on the way. What if you had fallen and broken a leg? Or your back? Did you think about that? You can't take those kinds of risks anymore.

"You need to grow up and face responsibility."

The Lie

Did Crystal lie? If so, how? The answer is yes. She lied in thinking that when men settle down and become responsible they should quit taking risks, that they should become nice and safe. She didn't realize that in their innermost being, men are adventurers. They need to take some risks. They need change. They need to push the envelope sometimes. That need flows from their core identity.

Behind the Lie

Some women think all men should act like women: safe, respectable, and nice. In truth, men have an innate need for a dash of adventure. They may not cross the prairies on horseback or face down an outlaw on a Dodge City street, but a yearning for adventure lies deep within them. At the same time, women have a need for security that runs just as deep in their being, and it also flows from their core identity. Problems arise when these two paradoxical needs collide.

Two couples met while on a Caribbean cruise, and hit it off well. One day the wives hit the shops while the men rented a small sailboat. Unfortunately, a storm blew in after several hours and brought a lot of rain with it. The guys got chilled and had to fight the storm all the way back to port. They finally tied up at the dock. Drenched and tired, one man said to the other, "Got a little rough out there, didn't it?"

The other man grinned and replied, "Yeah, but it sure beat shopping!"

The more we understand some of the basic differences between men and women, the better we can work through them. Let's explore how a couple can balance security and adventure.

WIVES NEED SECURITY

The 1969 film *Paint Your Wagon*[1] tells of a rollicking 1853 mining town in California and marvelously depicts the clash between the masculine need for adventure and the feminine need for security. Ben Rumson, played by Lee Marvin, represents the somewhat overdrawn masculine side, and his wife, Elizabeth, played by Jean Seberg, represents the feminine side.

In one of her songs, "A Million Miles Away Behind the Door," she expresses that need for home and security: "The sky is much too high to shelter me when darkness falls. Four cabin walls would be just right for me."[2]

That song flows from the centrality of relationships for women, because it is impossible for a woman to connect and stay connected with people if she has to move all the time, if uncertainty fills her life. When Crystal heard about Chad climbing that rock, she saw it as a reckless little boy act, one that threatened some important dimensions of security for her. Security needs seem to congregate in four basic arenas with women.

Marriage leads the list. If relationships form the core of life for women, then they place marriage at the very center of them all. When wives feel secure in their marriages, when they are assured that their husbands have made an unconditional commitment to them, that their husbands genuinely desire and strive to meet their needs, then that commitment and desire meets their prime need of security, and they can accept more uncertainty in other areas of their lives.

About ten years ago, we had just gone through some difficult times in our marriage, and we were exploring a ministry opportunity in Arizona, about four hundred miles away from home and family. I (Sheila) felt quite uneasy about this situation, since we'd worked through some of the issues, but I didn't feel totally secure yet. Because of my insecurity, Tim chose to pass up the opportunity.

More recently, Tim was offered a job in Colorado, an even greater distance from family. But I told him I'd consider it, because I felt much more secure in our marriage by that time. My response kind of surprised me, to be honest, since moving away from our grandchildren would have been tough on me.

Other *key relationships* come next. Extended family and friends play an important role in the lives of most women. One condition that I (Sheila) had if we moved to Colorado was that Tim had to fly me back once a month to see our kids and grandkids. Wives need to feel secure that they have other important relationships besides the one with their mates. Not long after we moved to Fallbrook, California, we talked to a number of couples who'd moved there about the same time we did. In nearly every case, the wives disliked the move at first, because it took them too far from key people in their lives. Once they built new connections, they fell in love with the area, but they struggled with leaving the connections they had already established.

Finances provide another area of security. A reliable, steady stream of income tends to help wives relax. A lot of husbands prefer entrepreneurial or sales jobs because they provide more of a challenge and greater opportunity for success and money, but many wives find the uncertainty of such positions threatening. The overall income may be greater, but they can't count on its regularity.

Housing not only provides an opportunity for wives' creativity, it also reinforces their nesting traits, their desire to have a home for the all-important family. Elizabeth in *Paint Your Wagon* sang about this aspect of security.

HUSBANDS NEED ADVENTURE

Ben Rumson had a different perspective. His theme song, "A Wanderin' Star," proclaimed the masculine ethos: "Wheels are made for rollin', mules are made to pack. I've never seen a sight that didn't look better looking back."[3] He founded a town when he struck gold, but when the gold played out he wanted to move on.

John Eldredge, in his book *Wild at Heart*[4], suggested that this difference in the male and female natures flows from Creation. God created Adam outside the Garden of Eden, in the wilderness, and then placed him in the Garden. But he created Eve within the Garden. Wildness seems to resonate with men, whether physical, emotional, or intellectual.

This characteristic also flows from the basic nature of males. Men derive the bulk of their self-esteem from accomplishment; they're task oriented. They test themselves against society, other men, and even themselves. We previously mentioned how Deborah Tannen, a communication researcher, concluded that men use conversation as competition, to see how they rank against others. The need for adventure and something new touches men in three main areas.

Physical activity leads the list. This activity can involve sports, camping, hunting, fishing, skydiving, you name it. At the age of forty-five, I (Tim) was invited by a friend to play in The Over the Hill Pigskin Shootout. The charity football game featured men at least thirty years old playing tackle, with pads, announcers, cheerleaders, "the whole enchilada." Nearly all had played football in college; several had played in the National Football League.

I loved the physical testing of myself against those guys, nearly all of whom were younger than I was. And, I found that I was competitive with them; I didn't get outclassed. I started two of the three games I played in, and we won two and tied one. That competitive streak in men helps us keep track! In one game I played a blocking tight end and went up against a friend in our church. Dan had grown up next door to me in Long Beach, outweighed me by a good thirty pounds, and had ten fewer years than I did. But I held him off. Man, that felt great.

I'll admit I felt very sore for a number of days afterward, but I considered it well worth it. Sheila thought it was crazy.

Change comes next. Whether it involves taking a new job, moving to a new area, or just thinking about these ventures, change stimulates men. Change offers a challenge, a way to get out of the rut. In the week we wrote this chapter, I (Tim) met with a friend from high school days who now lives in France and works with a business college. He's had the same position for about ten years now, loves what he does, and makes good money. But he recently told his boss, "I'm stale. I can do this in my sleep. You need to find something different for me or I'll go crazy."

We've seen how wives' need for security contrasts with their husbands' need for adventure. How do men react when their wives try to deny or restrict their need for adventure?

On the Receiving End

Chad deeply resented Crystal's comments about his taking risks on the fishing trip. He was responsible. He had some good insurance coverage to handle the finances if he got hurt. He worked hard at his job. He made sure they paid all the bills and had a good life. But he also needed some opportunities to relax, to blow off steam, to play. Men typically respond in several ways when their wives want them to ignore this need. Some will ignore the pressure from their wives; others will give in to it.

Identity confusion may head this list of male responses. Men sense their primal need for adventure, risk, and change, yet feel pressure from society and spouses to be responsible and act grown up, to be nice and respectable. They want to be a little dangerous and unpredictable, but they don't know how to express that desire. They don't quite know what it means to be a man. Society's changing male and female roles over the last thirty years have made it difficult for men to clarify the masculine identity.

Overcompensation with foolishly risky behaviors comes next on the list. A variety of counterfeit adventures entice men, but they don't deliver satisfaction, only more frustration. Frustrated men sometimes turn to pornography, marital affairs, excessive drinking, and workaholism in a vain attempt to feed their male soul.

Apathy hits too many men. They become bored with a passive life and withdraw. They accept the death of their dreams. They fear they will never live out their dreams of adventure, and so they give up the goal. They go through the motions of life; they may even do all the right things. But autopilot has taken over control.

Frustration at the identity confusion can grow into *anger* and may spill out with just a minor provocation. Road rage has become commonplace, and husbands too often strike out verbally or physically at their wives and others. They abuse their God-given strength because they haven't found the right outlet for it. So how do we balance these different and seemingly conflicting needs of husbands and wives?

Living the Truth

We begin by understanding that men and women have significant differences and that both security and adventure are good, but can be misused. Let's see what the Word of God says about these two traits.

GODLY SECURITY

Both husbands and wives need to develop a solid sense of security, a security that touches both physical and relational needs. God created us with physical needs, and he wants us to find security in having them met, as his Son Jesus told us: "So don't worry about having enough food or drink or clothing. Why be like the pagans who are so deeply concerned about these things? Your heavenly Father already knows all your needs" (Matthew 6:31-32 NLT).

God knows that we have physical needs. He also knows that we have relational needs, and he begins to meet them by offering us a permanent relationship with him, promising us, "Never will I leave you; never will I forsake you" (Hebrews 13:5).

He designed marriage to provide a lifetime of security. When the Pharisees asked Jesus about divorce and the permanency of marriage, he responded,

> "Haven't you read," he replied, "that at the beginning the Creator 'made them male and female,' and said, 'For this reason a man will leave his father and mother and be united to his wife, and the two will become one flesh'? So they are no longer two, but one. Therefore what God has joined together, let man not separate." (Matthew 19:4-6)

He also gave us the opportunity to develop friendships that we can count on. "A friend loves at all times, and a brother is born for adversity" (Proverbs 17:17).

Let's realize that wanting to have our needs met is godly! But the way we try to build security may not be.

SEDUCTIVE SECURITY

We make a major mistake when we expect that accumulating the stuff of life will provide the security that we'll continue to have the stuff of life. God knows that we have physical needs, but he wants us to trust him, not the accumulation of things, to insure provision for those needs. Proverbs 11:28 (NLT) tells us clearly, "Trust in your money and down you go! But the godly flourish like leaves in spring."

We found a great number of passages that support that truth. If you are interested in this subject, you may want to read Job 31:24-28, Psalm 52:7-9, Matthew 6:25-34, Luke 12:15-21, Romans 8:24-25, 2 Corinthians 5:7, and 1 Timothy 6:17.

Let's go back and read all of a verse we quoted only

partially earlier, because it provides the greater picture of where we ultimately gain security. "Keep your lives free from the love of money and be content with what you have, because God has said, 'Never will I leave you; never will I forsake you'" (Hebrews 13:5). We don't have to rely on money to build a sense of security, because God promises his permanent presence in our lives.

Let's take another trip back to another passage we quoted only partially earlier. In Matthew 6:31-32, we read that God knows about our physical needs. Now, read those verses again along with verse 33 (NLT):

> "So don't worry about having enough food or
> drink or clothing. Why be like the pagans who
> are so deeply concerned about these things?
> Your heavenly Father already knows all your
> needs, and he will give you all you need from
> day to day if you live for him and make the
> Kingdom of God your primary concern."

Notice that God gives us all we need "from day to day." We don't need to trust in storing up stuff; we just need to trust in God and make him our primary concern. Security seduces us when we trust in anything other than God for the meeting of our needs. Of course, we do our part: we work, and we prepare for the future. God's Word, especially Proverbs, tells us to be wise stewards of the stuff of life. But we must also avoid the seduction of trusting in that stuff.

GODLY RISK

Risk seems like an inherent component of life, doesn't it? We may try to minimize it, but at the same time we shouldn't necessarily try to avoid it entirely. God takes risks. He risked having a relationship with us when he gave us free will. When Jesus said that few enter through the narrow gate that leads to life, but that many enter through the wide gate that leads to destruction (see Matthew 7:13-14), he indicated that when God took that chance, he lost more people than he gained.

Gideon risked embarrassment, defeat, and death when he

whittled his army of thirty-two thousand down to three hundred at God's command. (See Judges 6:11–7:8.) David risked his life and the lives of his people when he accepted the challenge of fighting a giant, more than nine feet tall, with no armor for protection and armed with nothing but a slingshot. (See 1 Samuel 17.) Abram took a risk when he was obedient to God's command to leave his home and family to go to a land he didn't know anything about, and which God didn't even identify. (See Genesis 12:1–4.)

Consistently, God asks us to do things even though we don't know how they will turn out. Read the following passages and meditate on them to get a sense of the risks we take in following his Son Jesus.

> But hope that is seen is no hope at all. Who hopes for what he already has? But if we hope for what we do not yet have, we wait for it patiently. (Romans 8:24–25)

> So we fix our eyes not on what is seen, but on what is unseen. (2 Corinthians 4:18)

> Now faith is being sure of what we hope for and certain of what we do not see. (Hebrews 11:1)

Please grab onto the truth set forth in these verses: the only certainty in this life is God. As he did with Abraham, he consistently asks us to take risks in which we can't see the final outcome of our obedience. The only way we can do that is by doing what Abraham did—trusting that whatever happens, in the end God always wins. But not all risk is godly and wise.

UNGODLY RISK

Godly risk has nothing to do with irresponsibility. Godly risk responds to the uncertainty of life with trust in God, specifically certainty in the areas in which God tells us we can trust him. Quitting our job and "trusting in the Lord" to provide for our needs isn't godly risk but laziness, stupidity, and tempting

God. "If anyone does not provide for his relatives, and especially for his immediate family, he has denied the faith and is worse than an unbeliever" (1 Timothy 5:8). "Do not put the Lord your God to the test" (Luke 4:12). That's pretty clear, isn't it?

Real men live up to their responsibilities. They don't get flaky and untrustworthy. They don't pursue adventure and change at the expense of meeting the basic needs of their families.

Godly risk also doesn't encourage men to pursue their dream in a selfish manner that leads them away from God. Living adventurously means taking risks to follow God, not to follow selfish desires. The biblical character Cain provides repeated examples of taking risks in order to serve self.

First, he took the risk of sacrificing to God contrary to what God requested. When he came out second best in comparison to his brother Abel, he killed him. God then told him the consequences of taking that risk: "When you work the ground, it will no longer yield its crops for you. You will be a restless wanderer on the earth" (Genesis 4:12).

How did Cain respond to that pronouncement? Once again, he took the risk of doing what he wanted instead of what God wanted. Rather than being a "restless wanderer," as God had prophesied he would be, just four verses later, Cain settled down. "So Cain went out from the LORD's presence and lived in the land of Nod, east of Eden. Cain lay with his wife, and she became pregnant and gave birth to Enoch. Cain was then *building a city*" (Genesis 4:16–17).

Ungodly risks include stupid acts. Some things just shouldn't even be considered because they're just too dangerous. When we do something reckless and then ask God to bail us out of the mess we've made, we are tempting God. We've seen churches take risks with building programs that they couldn't possibly complete, using the reason, "We're stepping out on faith that God will provide." Well, unless God has clearly and specifically told them to do that, they're tempting God, which is just plain stupid.

Men do that with a variety of behaviors. They open

themselves up to needless temptation; they take business risks, and they jeopardize their personal lives and the lives of their families. So husband, realize that God did put a need for adventure and change within you, but also realize that how you express that need may go beyond what God intended.

STRIKE A BALANCE

Keep in mind that husbands don't necessarily express irresponsibility when they seek adventure, and that wives don't necessarily mistrust God when they desire security. God placed both of those needs and desires within them. Think of these two traits as different ends of a continuum. The glory comes as husbands and wives dance between them both, together.

Every couple will strike a different balance. Husbands vary in how much adventure and change they yearn for, just as wives vary in how much security they yearn for. The degrees of each will change over the years. But each marriage partner needs to have a deep concern for the other, being careful not to insist on getting their own way to the detriment of the other.

We think we can give a good scriptural example of that truth. Let's go back to the Creation narrative.

> Then God said, "Let us make people in our image, to be like ourselves. They will be masters over all life—the fish in the sea, the birds in the sky, and all the livestock, wild animals, and small animals." So God created people in his own image; God patterned them after himself; male and female he created them. God blessed them and told them, "Multiply and fill the earth and subdue it. Be masters over the fish and birds and all the animals." (Genesis 1:26–28 NLT)

What an adventure! To explore the earth, to fill it, to take control of it. What a *masculine* adventure! Oh really? To whom did God give that adventure? To *both* men and women. He created them both in his image. Together they are to carry out that adventure.

But they each have different roles in the adventure. Exploring the earth isn't enough. Once that's been done, it needs to be tamed, subdued, settled, civilized, developed. All that requires putting down roots. And the result of putting down roots? Security.

Yes, men can go overboard with adventure. And women can go overboard with security. But together, they can carry out God's plan for humanity. And that's the truth.

Notes

LIE 2

1. Dr. Laura Schlessinger, *The Proper Care and Feeding of Husbands* (New York: HarperCollins, 2004).

2. Dr. James Dobson, *Focus on the Family Marriage Ministry Group Starter Kit* (Ventura, Cali.: Regal Books: Book & Video edition, June 2003).

3. Dr. Laura Schlessinger, *The Proper Care and Feeding of Husbands* (New York: HarperCollins, 2004).

4. Dr. Gary and Barbara Rosberg, *5 Love Needs of Men and Women* (Carol Stream, Ill.: Tyndale House Publishers, 2001).

LIE 3

1. Maggie Gallagher and Linda Waite, *The Case for Marriage* (New York: Broadway, 2001).

LIE 4

1. Maxine Hanks quoted in Kristen Moulton, "Baptists, Mormons Share Some Views," Salt Lake City, June 11, 1998, © Associated Press.

2. Winston Churchill, October 1, 1939.

3. Dr. Gary and Barbara Rosberg, *5 Love Needs of Men and Women* (Carol Stream, Ill.: Tyndale House Publishers, 2001).

4. Maggie Gallagher, as cited in David Blankenhorn, Don S. Browning, Mary Stewart Van Leeuwen, *Does Christianity Teach Male Headship? The Equal-Regard Marriage and Its Critics* (Grand Rapids, Mich.: Wm. B. Eerdmans Publishing Company, 2004).

L,IE 6

1. Elisabeth Noelle-Neumann, *The Spiral of Silence*, 2d ed. (Chicago: University of Chicago Press, 1991).

2. Rachel Rosenfeld, "Self-Disclosure Avoidance: Why I Am Afraid to Tell You Who I Am," *Communication Monographs* 46 (1979): 64–74 (Washington, D.C.: National Communication Association; http://www.natcom.org/pubs/journal_history.htm).

L,IE 7

1. J. Holmes, as cited in Joseph A. DeVito, *Human Communication* (Boston: Allyn & Bacon, 2002).

2. Rachel Rosenfeld, as cited in DeVito.

3. Dr. Laura Schlessinger, *The Proper Care and Feeding of Husbands* (New York: HarperCollins, 2004).

L,IE 8

1. *Merriam-Webster's Collegiate Dictionary*, 10th ed. (Springfield, Mass: Merriam-Webster, 2002).

2. WordNet 2.0, http://www.cogsci.princeton.edu/cgibin/webwn2.0?stage=1&word=intimacy.

3. Dr. James Dobson, *Focus on the Family Marriage Ministry Group Starter Kit* (Ventura, Cali.: Regal Books: Book & Video edition, June 2003).

4. I. Altman and D. Taylor, *Social Penetration: The Development of Interpersonal Relationships* (New York: Holt, Rinehart and Winston, 1973).

L<small>IE</small> 10

1. Deborah Tannen, *Gender and Discourse* (New York: Oxford University Press; 1995 edition).

2. Dr. Cynthia Torppa, quoted in *Gender and Discourse* (New York: Oxford University Press; 1995 edition).

3. Deborah Tannen, *You Just Don't Understand* (New York: Perennial Currents, 2001).

4. Deborah Tannen, *Talking from 9 to 5* (New York: Quill, 1995).

5. Dr. Laura Schlessinger, *The Proper Care and Feeding of Husbands* (New York: HarperCollins, 2004).

6. Joseph A. DeVito, *Human Communication* (Boston: Allyn & Bacon, 2002).

7. Ibid.

L<small>IE</small> 11

1. Dr. Gary and Barbara Rosberg, *5 Love Needs of Men and Women* (Carol Stream, Ill.: Tyndale House Publishers, 2001).

2. Dr. Laura Schlessinger, *The Proper Care and Feeding of Husbands* (New York: HarperCollins, 2004).

3. Joseph C. Dillow, *Solomon on Sex* (Nashville: Thomas Nelson, Inc., 1982).

4. Ibid.

LIE 12

1. *Paint Your Wagon*, DVD directed by Joshua Logan (1969; Los Angeles, CA: Paramount Home Video, 2002).

2. Frederick Loewe, *A Million Miles Away Behind the Door*, 1969. Lyrics: Alan Jay Lerner. This song is part of the *Paint Your Wagon* musical score.

3. Frederick Loewe, *A Wanderin' Star,* 1952. Lyrics: Alan Jay Lerner. This song is part of the *Paint Your Wagon* musical score.

4. John Eldredge, *Wild at Heart* (Nashville: Nelson Books, 2001).

Readers' Guide

For Personal Reflection
or Group Discussion

Readers' Guide

The following questions are designed to be a resource tool that promotes small-group discussion, reflection, and personal application. You may use them in a variety of settings, including a women's Sunday school class, retreat, neighborhood women's group, and so forth.

You may also use these questions on your own, adapting them to your particular situation.

Some questions may seem pretty easy to answer; others may be quite personal and challenging. Prayerfully ask God to use them according to his will in your marriage and the marriages of others. Ask him for wisdom in recognizing some of your patterns of relating to your spouse—and for the desire to make any necessary changes in attitude and action.

Open up your heart and mind to new, godly ways of thinking, feeling, and responding to your spouse and God. Be willing to strengthen weak areas of your relationship and to rejoice in and build on stronger areas.

Perhaps your husband (or future husband) will be interested in discussing aspects of these chapters with you (or even reading them himself). Maybe he won't … at least right now. Either way, accept the exciting challenge of answering these questions and doing what you can, in God's power, to face any lies that are keeping your marriage from being the best it can be.

All of us—wives and husbands—have room for

improvement in our marriage relationships. Praise God that he loves each of us, provides his Spirit to empower and guide us, and cares deeply about each of our marriages. He created marriage! And, as the authors freely share, he loves to work small and large miracles in our lives!

LIE ONE: I LOVE YOU JUST THE WAY YOU ARE

1. Why is it easy to overlook or minimize a man's (or woman's) faults during dating?

2. As the story of Krista and Joel illustrated, what kinds of things happen when we have "hidden agendas" for our spouses, trying to change them into becoming more like who we want them to be? How might you respond if someone tried to change you—to make you a "project"? Why?

3. Is it possible to truly accept your spouse just as he is, yet encourage him to become the best man and husband he can be? Explain your answer.

4. What's the difference between a sin and a quirk in a husband's life? Why is it important for his wife to understand the difference?

5. What role does forgiveness play in the acceptance of a spouse?

6. What keeps spouses from being forgiving? And what does unforgiveness create?

7. According to the authors, which sinful choices need to be faced head-on in a marriage? Why, in these situations, must husbands face the logical consequences of their decisions?

8. If you begin to thank God for your husband's quirks, what might happen? How do you feel about this?

LIE 2: I'LL ALWAYS RESPECT YOU

1. Read the Amplified Bible's translation of Ephesians 5:33 on page 36. What light does this verse shed on what it means to "respect"

your husband? What did you feel and think as you read this? Why?

2. What are some practical ways in which wives can show respect and appreciation for their husbands?

3. As you read some of the husbands' perspectives, what came to mind? How can wives nurture their husbands more effectively?

4. The authors wrote, "Typically when husbands don't get their needs met, they decrease their efforts to meet the needs of their wives. They divest themselves emotionally from the relationship, hoping to cut their losses." If you feel comfortable sharing, talk about a time when this occurred in your marriage.

5. "Sometimes we give respect based on the position," the authors wrote, "not the perfection of the recipient." What does this mean, within the context of a marital relationship? Consider what 1 Peter 2:18 reveals about this issue.

6. Which of the five basic steps in expressing respect comes easiest to you? Which one is the hardest? Why?

7. Define what it means to "listen actively." Is this easy or difficult for you? Why?

LIE 3: I'LL LOVE YOU FOR RICHER OR FOR POORER

1. Why are issues of finances often a source of marital conflict?

2. What were your expectations concerning your husband's ability to provide for you financially? How have they affected your marriage in positive or negative ways?

3. As you read about the benefits of spending money, which one(s) hits close to home? Why? Which factors have contributed to how you spend money? To how your husband spends money?

4. To what degree does our upbringing influence our view of money? If you feel comfortable doing so, share an example from your life.

5. What finance-related stresses affect the marriages of people you know? Affect your own marriage?

6. How important is marital trust when financial issues surface? Why?

7. What can a married couple do when money-related issues cause friction? Feel free to share an example from your life.

LIE 4: YOU AREN'T MY BOSS

1. When you read the word *submission*, what did you feel? Why?

2. Why does the principle of submission sometimes create such struggles within marriages today?

3. In what ways does submission contradict our culture's view of individualism?

4. Why must husbands and wives address submission-related issues? Which specific consequences, according to the authors, result when biblical submission is lacking?

5. What submission-related tensions have surfaced in your marriage or the marriage of someone you know well? What happened? How has your husband (or your friend's husband) responded?

6. "Submission involves much more than wives submitting to their husbands," the authors wrote. Discuss the following:
   - Jesus' submission to the Father (Hebrews 5:7)
   - Christians' submission to God (James 4:7)
   - Christians' submission to one another (Ephesians 5:18–21)
   - Church members' submission to their spiritual leaders (Hebrews 13:17)
   - Christians' submission to the government (Romans 13:1–3)
   - Wives' submission to their husbands (Ephesians 5:21–22)

7. Why is it important for husbands to sacrifice and for wives to submit? How do these patterns complement each other to create balance and harmony?

LIE 5: I'LL NEVER BE UNFAITHFUL TO YOU

1. What, according to the authors, is unfaithfulness to one's spouse?

2. Which of the three forms of adultery may occur most frequently in your circle of relationships? Why is it important for each of us to guard against all three forms?

3. What key point(s) stood out to you concerning the reasons why Christian women break their marriage vows?

4. Why is "adultery of the heart" so damaging?

5. In our culture today, what types of things foster a climate in which "adultery by neglect" can occur? What can we do to counteract these things?

6. Why it is important to use God's wisdom to examine your life ruthlessly, recognize danger zones, and discover how you can protect yourself? Why do some people avoid doing this?

7. What does it mean to "guard" our hearts, as Proverbs 4:23 mentions? What kinds of sacrifices might we have to make in order to escape strong temptations?

LIE 6: NOTHING'S WRONG; I'M JUST FINE

1. What's the difference between the "direct" and "indirect" messages we send our spouses? What are their advantages? Their disadvantages? What kind of messages do you send most often?

2. As you read reasons why wives use indirect communication, which reason(s) jumped out at you? Describe a time when you used indirect communication with your spouse—and perhaps why you did it.

3. What, according to the Bible, is God's communication pattern? What's an example of how highly he values effective communication?

4. If you could offer your husband (or prospective husband) one tip on what he could do to create a better communication "safe zone" for you, what would you say? How might you communicate this to him in a way he can receive positively, with understanding?

5. What might you do to help establish a "common language" with your spouse?

6. Paul wrote about "speaking the truth in love." What does this phrase mean? Give an example or two from your life.

LIE 7: I DON'T NEED YOUR HELP; I CAN TAKE CARE OF IT

1. Why is it important for wives to spell out specific requests of their husbands?

2. What is "self-disclosure hesitancy," and why does it occur?

3. Based on your experience, do you agree with the authors that "women have better communication skills than men do"? Why or why not? If this is true, what can happen when wives think their husbands should somehow know and respond to their often unspoken desires and dreams?

4. What can wives do to get their desires and requests across to their more fact-oriented husbands? What kinds of things work? Which ones don't? (Feel free to share a funny or serious story.)

5. Review the four steps to better communication between wives and their husbands. Which one is the hardest for you to apply? Which one is the easiest? Why?

6. If a critical spirit has taken root, what can we do about it?

LIE 8: WE JUST DON'T HAVE ANYTHING IN COMMON ANYMORE

1. Do you think every person has a need to connect with someone on an intimate level? Explain your answer.

2. Is it right for a wife to expect her husband to meet most of her needs for intimacy? Why or why not?

3. What, according to the authors, are the three main factors that cause wives to expect so much intimacy from their husbands?

4. What benefits accrue when a wife and her husband deliberately commit themselves to sharing more time and activities together?

5. Although we desire intimacy, what kinds of things do we do to protect our innermost person—thereby hindering the development of intimacy?

6. Discuss how you, or others you know, have developed sources of intimacy that supplement the intimacy that marriage can provide. Use the following as a guide:

   a. God

   b. Friends

   c. Mentors

7. How committed are you to using the authors' three suggestions for building deeper intimacy with your spouse—spending significant time together; investing time in conversation; developing common activities? What obstacles will you have to overcome in order to do each of these three things?

LIE 9: DO I LOOK GOOD IN THIS DRESS?

1. Describe a time when you asked your husband if he liked an outfit you were wearing. What were you really asking?

2. To what degree do you think women derive their sense of self-worth and self-image from their appearance? How does this relate to 1 Peter 3:3–4?

3. Why do you think the authors focused on this particular lie? Is it really as prominent as they think it is? Explain your answer.

4. If you ask for your husband's honest opinion and you don't like what you hear (and make that point clear!), what are you really

doing—to yourself and to him? Why, as the authors emphasize, is it important to "cherish truthful answers"?

5. What might you to do help your husband answer your questions truthfully, but in love, especially if he tends to give insensitive answers? (See Ephesians 4:15.)

6. On a scale of one to ten, with one being the lowest, how often does your husband affirm your physical attractiveness? How do you feel as a result? (Be as honest as you can.)

LIE 10: YOU NEVER TALK TO ME

1. Which factors, such as work responsibilities or children, make it hard for you and your spouse to talk about your relationship? How do you feel about this?

2. How do men tend to use conversation, as opposed to how women use it?

3. Why is it important for us to understand the ways in which husbands' communication style differ from wives' communication style?

4. Describe a time when you and your husband experienced tension because of your differing communication styles. How did you resolve things? What did you learn from that experience?

5. As you read the specific listening skills husbands and wives can use to enhance their conversations, which ones gave you "Aha" moments? Which ones do you already practice? Which ones are lacking?

6. Think about how the following skills might help you to improve your communication with your husband:

   a. Openness—sharing information about yourselves (feelings, thoughts, joys, struggles)

   b. Positiveness—truly caring about the other person and your relationship; not having critical and negative attitudes toward your spouse

c. Immediacy—linking with the other person (eye contact, physical closeness)

7. How might what you read in this chapter affect the way you approach conversations with your husband this coming week? What might you do differently? Be as specific as you can as you share ideas.

LIE 11: NOT TONIGHT, DEAR; I HAVE A HEADACHE

1. How do husbands feel, according to the authors, when their wives continue to withhold sex from them? What did you think as you read about this?

2. If you feel comfortable doing so, share reasons why you have put off having sex with your husband sometimes.

3. What happens when sexual intimacy in marriage is denied for periods of time, even months or years?

4. Reread 1 Corinthians 7:3-5. What do these verses reveal?

5. The authors suggested talking frankly with your husband about his sexual needs and desires. What do you think about this? What might the benefits be? What risks might be involved?

6. How important is nonsexual touch to you? What can a wife do to encourage her husband to demonstrate more affection during the day?

7. If more wives realized that their husbands equated sex with intimate connection with them, how might their bedroom activities change? Why?

LIE 12: YOU NEED TO GROW UP AND FACE RESPONSIBILITY

1. Why is it important to realize that husbands need to have "adventures" from time to time?

2. In your experience, what happens when the husband's need for adventure collides with your need for security?

3. The authors wrote, "When wives feel secure in their marriages, when they are assured that their husbands have made an unconditional commitment to them, that their husbands genuinely desire and strive to meet their needs, then ... they can accept more uncertainty in other areas of their lives." Do you agree or disagree with this statement? Why? Feel free to share from your experience.

4. Contrast your need for security with your husband's likely need for adventure. In what way(s) are you different or similar in the following areas:

   a. Need for physical activity (camping, sports, hunting, and so forth)

   b. Need for change (new job, new challenge, new location, and so forth)

5. What did the authors mean by the phrase "seductive security"? Why do so many people today equate "stuff" with security? How does the accumulation of stuff relate to the trust God desires that we place in him day to day?

6. Why is it important to know the difference between "godly risk" and "ungodly risk" when evaluating your husband's desires for risk and adventure? What are those differences?

7. What can you and your spouse do, on a regular basis, to demonstrate concern for the adventure, change, and/or security you each yearn for?